"My friend Paul-Gordon Chandler leads us around the world and introduces us to the Christians with whom we'll worship the Lord in heaven someday. During the journey we discover how much we need one another in the body of Christ."

LUIS PALAU, *evangelist*

"I really liked this book because Paul-Gordon Chandler shows us mission work at its best. It is a style of ministry that is marked by listening and learning from indigenous Christians. It is about partnering with Christians from around the world in the task of contextualizing the gospel."

TONY CAMPOLO, *Eastern College, St. Davids, Pennsylvania*

"Yes, learn! Especially from Christians who have paid the price for their faith. I know of no greater theme today to make known our church. Wholeheartedly recommended!"

BROTHER ANDREW, *founder, Open Doors*

"I have personally benefited from reading this book. My own spirit has been broadened, and I have pleasure and less concern about Christians whose personalities and temperaments differ from mine— they are wonderful brothers of the Lord."

KENNETH N. TAYLOR, *chairman, Tyndale House Publishers*

"Some men write about the world. Others write about God. Paul-Gordon Chandler does both, and in one book! He manages to entice you into the cultures of the nations, creating a beautiful tapestry that is woven with threads drawn from different aspects of the character of God.

"Paul's journeys in the nations of the earth read like a series of divinely connected relationships that at once enchants and inspires the reader. You fall in love with the church of Jesus Christ all over again as a result of reading *God's Global Mosaic.*

"Paul's record is both inspirational and informational, and leaves the reader with a greater vision of God's glory in the church and the peoples of the earth."

FLOYD MCCLUNG, *author and former executive director of international operations, Youth With A Mission*

"Churches with white steeples, people arranged in orderly pews, choruses of 'Rock of Ages' and 'Great Is Thy Faithfulness'—this is often the limited view Americans have of the Christian faith. In *God's Global Mosaic*, Paul-Gordon Chandler reveals a broader, richer and compelling view of the Christian faith as a world-wide faith; a view that speaks to the bigness of God and the diversity of his purposes for all the nations."

RICHARD E. STEARNS, *president, World Vision*

"It is an unfortunate fact that the culture we live in determines much of how we read the Bible and even experience God. Fortunately, *God's Global Mosaic* takes off those cultural blinders and exposes us to the profound and sometimes provocative perspectives of non-Western Christians."

DR. WESLEY K. STAFFORD, *president, Compassion International*

"Throughout time the story has been the form by which we relate profound truth to one another. In *God's Global Mosaic*, Paul-Gordon Chandler relates stories that communicate the deep and multifaceted truths of men and women who experience the love of Christ and the grace of God as they follow him down very desperate paths of life. This pilgrimage is at the same time one, and yet strikingly unique. Paul captures the essence of both the oneness and the uniqueness."

PAUL MCKAUGHAN, *president/CEO,*
Evangelical Fellowship of Mission Agencies

"*God's Global Mosaic* is a refreshing original book. Chandler intellectually celebrates the beauty of world Christianity's diversity and unity. This should be required reading for anyone who purports to be a world Christian."

DR. LYLE W. DORSETT, *professor of Christian ministries*
and evangelism, Wheaton College

"If we are to arrive at the partnership model in world Christianity, Christians need to learn to appreciate the richness of Christianity in other cultures and approach Christians in these cultures with a desire for mutual enrichment. This book is a fine place to start such a learning process."

AJITH FERNANDO, *author, teacher and director of Youth for Christ,*
Sri Lanka

"Paul-Gordon Chandler, with a background of extensive world travels and experience, has remarkable sensitivities and unusual insights into other cultures. He has drawn creative lessons for the Christian life from observing the customs of Christians in many regions of the world. Christians in the West can profit immensely from the lessons given in this book."

DAVID M. HOWARD, *former international director, World Evangelical Fellowship*

"*God's Global Mosaic* is a wonderful tapestry of faith in God, who transcends the paradigms of culture and individual experience. This is a book that defines the term *world Christian*. My faith was challenged in reading *God's Global Mosaic*. There is much to be learned through people who know and experience God outside the familiar box of our own culture and background."

RON NIKKEL, *president, Prison Fellowship International*

"In this inspiring book Paul-Gordon Chandler, through his extensive travels and his natural identification with Christians on all continents, provides the reader with a unique perspective on what God is doing around the world. He gives us an appreciation for the varied 'flavors' of the gospel as it is expressed and lived out in very different contexts."

RAMEZ L. ATALLAH, *general secretary, Bible Society of Egypt*

God's Global
MOSAIC
What We Can Learn from Christians Around the World

Paul-Gordon Chandler
FOREWORD BY JOHN STOTT

InterVarsity Press
Downers Grove, Illinois

InterVarsity Press
P.O. Box 1400, Downers Grove, IL 60515
World Wide Web: www.ivpress.com
E-mail: mail@ivpress.com

InterVarsity Press® is the book-publishing division of InterVarsity Christian Fellowship/USA®, a student movement active on campus at hundreds of universities, colleges and schools of nursing in the United States of America, and a member movement of the International Fellowship of Evangelical Students. For information about local and regional activities, write Public Relations Dept., InterVarsity Christian Fellowship/USA, 6400 Schroeder Rd., P.O. Box 7895, Madison, WI 53707-7895.

All Scripture quotations, unless otherwise indicated, are taken from the Holy Bible, New International Version®. NIV®. *Copyright ©1973, 1978, 1984 by International Bible Society. Used by permission of Zondervan Publishing House. All rights reserved.*

First published in 1997 in Great Britain by SPCK/Triangle under the title Divine Mosaic.

Every effort has been made to trace and contact the copyright holder for the poem found on page 54. The author will be pleased to rectify any omission in future editions if notified by the copyright holder.

Cover photographs: Jim Whitmer (Indian girl); International Bible Society and Pioneers (all other photographs)

ISBN 0-8308-2251-8

Printed in the United States of America ∞

Library of Congress Cataloging-in-Publication Data

Chandler, Paul Gordon.
  God's global mosaic : what we can learn from Christians around the world/
Paul-Gordon Chandler.
    p. cm.
  Includes bibliographical references.
  ISBN 0-8308-2251-8 (pbk. : alk. paper)
  1. Christianity and culture. 2. Multiculturalism—Religious aspects—Christianity. I.
Title.
BR115.C8 C414 2000
270.8'2—dc21
                                                                        99-053606

20 19 18 17 16 15 14 13 12 11 10 9 8 7 6 5 4 3 2 1

16 15 14 13 12 11 10 09 08 07 06 05 04 03 02 01 00

*To Lynne, my wife, who to me displays
the beauty of God and the sweetness
of life as no one else,
and is the central and most important piece
in the divine mosaic of my life.*

CONTENTS

Acknowledgments

My thanks . . .

To Andrew T. LePeau, *the editorial director for InterVarsity Press, whom I have been privileged to work with.*

To the many Christians around the world *by whose faith and experience of God I have learned, grown and been changed, resulting in the shaping of my Christian life.*

To Partners International, *whose strategic international ministry gives me the honor of traveling and working with Christians all over the world.*

To my parents, Will and Nancy Chandler, *whose undying commitment and service to the existence of a strong indigenous church in Senegal, West Africa, provided me with what I consider to be one of the greatest of privileges—growing up in a foreign country.*

To my wife, Lynne, and my two children, Britelle and Treston, *for their endless encouragement, insight and inspiration during the writing of this book and their gracious sacrifice when I have had to be away overseas.*

Foreword

God's Global Mosaic is a remarkable combination of personal story, historical allusion, cultural reflection and biblical exposition. Paul-Gordon Chandler is a true internationalist, who has traveled the world with his ears and eyes wide open. While being committed to the unity of the gospel, he also describes the diversity of the church. He emphasizes reverence in Eastern Orthodoxy, perseverance in the Middle East, celebration in Latin America, liberation in Africa, the centrality of Christ in South Asia and the unpredictability of God in East Asia. His account is informed, thoughtful, devotional, sometimes humorous, always serious and challenging. One emerges from the reading with an enlarged vision of God.

John R. W. Stott
Rector Emeritus of All Souls Church,
Langham Place, London

Introduction

I once read that if the world were a small town of 1,000 people, it would include 564 Asians, 210 Europeans, 86 Africans, 80 South Americans and 60 North Americans. Its religions would work out at 300 Christians, 176 Muslims, 128 Hindus, 55 Buddhists and 47 animists.[1] Obviously, if we lived in a town with this diversity we could not afford to be monocultural and ethnocentric. We would have to adopt an attitude of sharing with and learning from others of different cultural backgrounds.

Just like this imaginary town, the church worldwide is an extremely diverse collection of people from every country, ethnic group and culture. Today's Christianity is a multicultural global movement that is polycentric and largely non-Western. It is like the canvas of a beautiful painting with contrasting and complementary colors. The foundation for our unity as Christians throughout the world is not our likeness but our diversity. Every time I travel to non-Western countries, I am reminded afresh of this world's amazing diversity. And this is perhaps most clearly seen through the cultural self-expressions of Christians throughout the world. Indigenous churches are bubbling over with their own spontaneous expressions of the Christian faith.

As God created each beautiful human face differently, it is safe to assume that he enjoys variety. There is one Christian faith, but many cultures. The gospel is one, but it finds expression in a variety of cultural forms as each individual's culture shapes both his or her response to Christ and understanding of the gospel. Consequently Christians around the world worship God in a variety of ways. The late Dr. D. T. Niles of Sri Lanka said:

> The Gospel is like a seed, and you have to sow it. When you sow the seed of the Gospel in Palestine, a plant that can be called Palestinian Christianity grows. When you sow it in Rome, a plant of Roman Christianity grows. You sow the Gospel in Great Britain and you get British Christianity. The seed of the Gospel is later brought to America, and a plant grows of American Christianity. Now, when missionaries come to our lands they brought not only the seed of the Gospel, but their own plant of Christianity, flower pot included! So, what we have to do is to break the flower pot, take out the seed of the Gospel, sow it in our own cultural soil, and let our own version of Christianity grow.[2]

I have written this book on the deep, twofold conviction that there can be no part of the worldwide church that is exclusively independent of the others and that our own Christian life is made more complete by learning from other cultural expressions of the Christian faith. These different expressions of the Christian faith must be in conversation with one another—for no one is closer to Jesus Christ than any other. The purpose of this book is to encourage Western Christians to learn about and benefit from the faith and experience of non-Western Christians. It is my hope that this book will encourage others to learn from Christians around the world.

This theme is very much part of my own spiritual journey. I spent the first eighteen years of my life in French-speaking West Africa, where I attended an international school made up of more than thirty nationalities. My after-school hours were largely spent with Senegalese, French and Lebanese friends from other schools, using the languages of French, Wolof and Arabic. Since then I have had the privilege of working with Christians throughout the world. This has made a deep impact on my spiritual life and growth. The exposure to the variety of Christian traditions around the world has served as a unique stimulus in clarifying and deepening my own Christian life and worship. My own ordination is a case in point: as an American from an evangelical background, I found myself in an Anglo-Catholic church in England kneeling before an Egyptian bishop who gave me a Jerusalem Bible in French as my ordination gift.

More than anything these experiences have demonstrated to me how Christianity worldwide is a *divine mosaic,* with each piece being a different cultural expression of the Christian faith, and the whole portraying the beauty of God's character as perhaps nothing else can. It is in our continual learning from these many cultural expressions of Christianity that our own faith can be made most complete.

When living near Carthage (in modern-day Tunisia) I developed an interest in ancient Christian mosaics. Some of the most beautiful examples there date from the time of Augustine, the bishop of Hippo and the North African early church. Yet today the beauty and glory of many of these tremendous mosaics has faded—not because of aging but due to individual pieces that have been lost. If we could only retrieve those pieces! In the same way, I see the church in any one culture—such as in the West—as an incomplete mosaic. In order to enhance the beauty and glory of our own faith and church we need to accept, grasp and apply this principle of learning from other cultural Christian expressions. This will allow us as Westerners to be receivers rather than (as has been traditionally the case) viewing ourselves primarily as providers. This is more pertinent than ever before, as opportunities increase for contact with Christians of other cultures and nationalities—due both to the developing multicultural dimension of many churches and to modern communications and travel possibilities. It is important that we build crosscultural relationships.

Like the world-famous *Magnum* photographer Abbas, who embarked on a pictorial essay of world Christianity, I aim to provide a unique glimpse of Christianity in six different parts of the world. However, it is important to mention that this book is not an analysis or critique of Christianity in each region; neither is it an anthropological study. Each of the first six chapters focuses on one prominent aspect of Christianity in a particular geographical region—an aspect from which Christians in the West can learn. The last chapter is a concluding perspective on our common crosscultural identity as Christians from different cultures, and the benefits of that identity.

I should also make clear that while my purpose here is to highlight positive traits that we can learn from the church around the world, it is not to idealize these other churches. I clearly recognize that they too, as we do in the West, have their own problems and weaknesses to work on. Additionally, as the goal is to emphasize one prominent Christian theme from each region, it is not possible in such brief chapters to explain all the exceptions that may exist within each area. I have purposely not included a chapter on the Western church. This is not because the church in the West is inferior and has nothing to offer—or because it is superior and therefore we evaluate all other parts of the church in the world to assimilate what is best into our own church while not having to ourselves be evaluated. Rather the reason is twofold. First, this book is specifically oriented to Western Christians to point out how we can benefit from Christians in other places around the world. Second, there is already a significant amount of material available on the Western church.

Each Christian theme highlighted in each region is based on scriptural illustrations that serve as the consistent foundation of that chapter. In this sense the overall aim of this book is devotional, encouraging Christian growth. Most important, these many and varied expressions of the Christian faith are *windows on God,* giving us a glimpse of God's understanding of perfection and completion in the new heaven and new earth that are to come. For as John recorded:

> I looked and there before me was a great multitude that no one could count, from every nation, tribe, people and language, standing before the throne and in front of the Lamb. (Rev 7:9)

A spectacular vision of the future that we can begin to experience in the present, seeing our God as never before.

> One Church in many, many places,
> One Faith with many, many faces,
> One World with many, many ways
> Of singing praises to the Lord of Life.[3]

—1—

A Deeper Dimension

Glimpsing His Majesty Through Eastern European Eyes

I *had passed KGB headquarters numerous times before. I had* even been inside one of the three massive buildings that made up this international powerhouse of espionage. I was well aware of all the dramatic political and spiritual changes taking place in the former Soviet Union. Yet nothing could have prepared me for what I was to see as I passed those buildings this time. In front of them the enormous statue of the founder of the KGB, Felix Dzerzhinsky, was no longer to be seen. Instead, positioned high on the podium where the statue formerly stood was a huge wooden cross. And painted in red across the foot of the podium were the words, "This is where real power is found."

Who could ever have foretold all the vast changes that took place in the Soviet Union in the early 1990s—central government collapsing, monuments to Lenin and Stalin felled and sold in Western black-market auctions around the world, Soviet Red Army paraphernalia sold to foreign tourists by the soldiers themselves? The West became obsessed with Soviet souvenirs, paying outrageous prices for cheap and inexpensive items, either because they bore a hammer and sickle or were made by someone who once had. Red Army badges, uniforms and watches, matryoshka stacking dolls, samovar teapots, gaudy balalaikas, Russian fur hats and black lacquered boxes—all had enormous prices and then depreciated just as quickly. These valued souvenirs quickly became so commonplace that they were seen simply as cheap trinkets.

Of the many Russian souvenirs and artifacts that were highly sought after, religious icons never lost their value. Rather, Russian icons are now worth more than ever in the auction houses. Beyond their artistic worth they stand as a symbol of Russian Christianity. Christians in the former Soviet Union describe their icons as "windows to heaven," enabling them to see God in new ways. The purpose of an icon is to see through it, beyond it, to the aspect of God and faith that it portrays.

The changes in both the former Soviet Union and Eastern Europe have enabled Christians from the West to glimpse the faith of Christians in this part of the world. And not only to glimpse their faith but to learn from it. The Christians in the former Soviet Union and Eastern Europe have served as windows to many of us from the West— through them we have seen God as never before, resulting in a deepening of our own Christian faith.

Standing in Awe of God

The first few years of the 1990s found me in Russia and Eastern Europe every few months, working alongside churches of every denomination—from the historic Russian Orthodox Church to unregistered house churches that during the Soviet era existed in secret. At that time I was working with an international Christian organization extensively involved in the development of indigenous Christian literature and Bible distribution in these countries.

On one of my earlier and longer visits to Russia my wife accompanied me. It happened to be during the middle of an infamous Russian winter, with a temperature average of –29°C (–20°F) during our two-month stay. How well we could understand Napoleon Bonaparte's comment on his defeat by the Russians: "a people who eat ice-cream [outdoors] in the winter cannot be defeated."

During that period, a typical workday would bring me back to the hotel at around 10 p.m., still not having eaten dinner. For the first few weeks the only apparent option for a convenient meal was the hotel restaurant. Yet the service was extremely poor and sometimes nonexistent—one night I literally had to beg the waiter to serve us. And out of a long and quite varied menu, only one item was ever available. The whole ordeal would typically take at least two hours, and as I was exhausted after long days of meetings all around the vast city of Moscow in sub-zero temperatures, this grew tiresome.

We then discovered a restaurant down the street within a five-minute walk from our hotel. It specialized in efficient service and was the perfect place to drop in and out for a quick meal. It was none other than the new Moscow Pizza Hut. We started frequenting Pizza Hut about every third night and did so for several weeks. We came to know the manager and almost all of the staff on a first-name basis. We did tire of pizza, but the restaurant's sheer convenience won out.

At first we were something of a novelty to the Pizza Hut staff. We were from the West; we were American; we spoke English. We had the feeling that they would have rolled out a red carpet for us had the restaurant not already had red carpeting. We were in many ways a mystery to them, and consequently they treated us with tremendous respect. However, after some time the mystery wore off, and we became commonplace. The respect and special treatment we had previously received greatly diminished—on one occasion when we stayed after eating to talk, they turned off the lamp above our table to let us know it was time to go home.

Something similar can happen in the Christian life. We have times when we stand in utter amazement of who God is, of all he has done and is doing in our lives. But then over time we lose the sense of awe and mystery, and our Christian life becomes commonplace; that special dynamic is missing. It all becomes too familiar, and that reverence or sense of awe, which the Bible calls "fearing God," no longer exists.

Among the amazing things that were taking place in Christian ministry in the former Soviet Union and Eastern Europe during the early 1990s, doors opened that had never before been open. There was an interest in and fascination with the Christian faith that I had never previously experienced and most probably will never experience again. I still find it difficult to describe the atmosphere of that period.

How can you explain the situation of a Russian minister I know who was marrying an average of sixteen couples every Sunday—yet he had married only three during the previous thirty years? People were literally flocking back to the church. Or how can I properly describe the scene in front of Moscow's McDonald's where I saw an old Russian woman, a babushka, receive a free Bible from a Christian group distributing the Scriptures? She sat down to read it on a park bench and was immediately approached by a young girl, dressed in black, with spiked hair and too many earrings and nose rings to count. This girl begged the elderly woman to give her the Bible. The woman held on to her new Bible ever more tightly as she shook her head back and forth. The girl then proceeded to take out money and asked if she could buy the Bible. The woman again refused and walked away, leaving the teenage girl still pleading for that book for which she so obviously longed.

How can I forget the time I came back to my hotel room in the middle of the day to find the cleaning lady lying down on my bed reading the Russian Bible I had left on the bedside table? Very much embarrassed, she apologized and left quickly, only to return immediately, offering what was to her a large sum of money to buy two Bibles, for herself and her friend. I gave her the Bibles at no cost— and a few minutes later there was a knock on my door. She and her friend, another cleaning lady, stood bearing two quite expensive and valued gifts for me: two super-size rolls of soft European toilet paper—very treasured and kept only for foreign VIPs, in contrast to the stiff crepe-paper-like equivalent used in Russia!

This atmosphere provided some unique opportunities—from interviews on Russian television and press conferences about the Christian faith to bringing together denominations that up to that point would not even stand in the same room together. It was exciting to experience these historic moments directly.

Yet paradoxically, in the midst of all that was taking place I experienced a profound emptiness, a void in my own spiritual journey. In the middle of seeing God do so much, I discovered I needed something more than even these wonderful experiences provided. I needed a fresh touch from him, a renewed glimpse of his face, a new sense of amazement of who he was. What I needed more than anything was to stand in awe of God once again, to have that tremendous sense of reverence for him.

Reverence for God is not something that Western Christianity strongly emphasizes. Instead the church in the West often de-emphasizes this aspect. Once when visiting a Christian bookshop in the United States, I saw a T-shirt for sale with the words, "Jesus Knows Diddley" ("nothing" in American slang) written across the front. My immediate thought was that whoever designed this T-shirt obviously does not know who Jesus is. Then I saw, written below in very small letters, "And Every Hair on Diddley's Head." I smiled, as most would. However, as I left that store I thought to myself, *Who-*

ever designed this shirt cannot hold Jesus in high regard because if
he did, he could not say something so incredibly irreverent.

I have found that Christians throughout the former Soviet Union
and Eastern Europe, whether Orthodox, Baptists or Pentecostals, are
supremely reverent toward God, showing him utmost respect and
therefore maintaining that sense of awe that I, along with many
Western Christians, lack. Whenever they pray outside a church service, such as before a meal, they always stand in his honor, even
when in public. In church, whenever possible, they kneel or bow in
reverence. They attend services to honor and adore the Almighty
that result in a profound seriousness in their attitude of worship. You
often see worshipers in tears.

Their church buildings offer inspiration to meditate on the majesty of God because of their sheer architectural beauty—the golden
onion-domes, the high ceilings, the expansive arches, all symboliz-
ing their emphasis on the royalty of God.

The history of Russia and the Russian Orthodox Church relates
directly to this. Indeed the Russian alphabet, the very foundation of
communication, originated from a desire to facilitate the worship of
God. In A.D. 860 Rastislav, Prince of Moravia (in the modern-day
Czech Republic), asked the Byzantine emperor, Michael III, to send
missionaries to instruct his people in the ways of the Christian God.
In response Patriarch Photius sent from Macedonia two Greek missionary brothers, Cyril and Methodius, who became known as the
"Apostles to the Slavs." They had grown up near the Slavs and knew
the Slavic language. As part of their mission they prepared an alphabet for this unwritten Slavic language so that the Slavs could have
the liturgy of worship in their native tongue. Eventually this script
was called Cyrillic—the alphabetic script still used in the former
Soviet Union—named after Cyril, the younger brother.

In 988 Prince Vladimir, from a place known at that time as
Kievan Rus, sent envoys to the Western church in Rome and to the

Eastern church in Constantinople (modern-day Istanbul). He knew he had to choose between one of these two divisions of Christianity or be brought under the influence of Islam coming from the south or the eastern religions coming westward. The story is told that his envoys, after visiting Rome, went to Constantinople. When they entered St. Sophia's Cathedral (Hagia Sophia, the Church of Holy Wisdom), they were so awestruck by its beauty and majestic atmosphere that they later said: "We knew not whether we were in heaven or on earth, for on earth there is no such splendour or beauty. . . . We knew only that God dwells there among men. . . . We can never forget that Beauty." Upon their return they reported this experience to Prince Vladimir, who on the basis of this story selected the Eastern church as the strain of Christianity his land would adopt. The word for Russian Orthodoxy in the language of Old Church Slavonic, which is still used today in church worship, is *Pravoslavie,* which means "true worship" or "right glory," reflecting the preeminence to a Russian Christian of reverence toward God.

All of this has led the Russian church to place a greater emphasis on worship than doctrine. As one Russian Christian wrote long ago: "Through heaven and earth, through wood and stone, through all creation visible and invisible, I offer veneration to the Creator and Master and Maker of all things."[1] Russian believers see themselves as supremely endowed with the task of worshiping God. And their worship is very much that of attending to Another—the Royal One, the King of kings. In the communion service celebrated nearly every week in Orthodox churches, before the Scripture is read the minister prays, "O Lord and Master, our God, who is in heaven has established the orders and armies of angels and archangels to minister to your majesty." Even the vestments of the ministers leading the worship services are reminiscent of royalty, denoting the royal presence of the Lord Jesus Christ.

The Glory and Mystery of God

The Bible is in essence a compilation of individuals' stories of faith and their experience of God. The stories are many and told in varying degrees of detail—yet it seems that Moses directly experienced more of God's spectacular demonstrations than anyone else mentioned in the Scriptures. If anyone had seen God supernaturally at work, it was Moses, from the outset of his life to its very end. We find him constantly standing in amazement in response to the actions of Almighty God. As a baby from a slave family in a foreign country, he narrowly escaped almost certain death thanks to the miraculous intervention of the daughter of the Egyptian Pharaoh. This resulted in his being raised as an Egyptian prince. Later we read about Moses in exile, about the burning bush that was not consumed by the flames and his shepherd's rod, which became a snake. On returning to Egypt to free his people, Moses initiated the series of plagues under God's direction. When on the run in the desert he experienced the opening of the Red Sea as a means of escape and was then led by the miraculous cloud during the day and the pillar of fire at night. While in the desert he saw the supernatural provision of food for the Israelites in the form of quail and manna. Water was provided when a poisonous lake was made drinkable and when a stream gushed from a rock. Seemingly impossible battles against the Amalekites were won under his leadership. God spoke with him on Mount Sinai and wrote the Ten Commandments for him. Moses did not live an ordinary life; it was truly extraordinary.

Yet there was quite obviously a time in Moses' life when he felt he needed more spiritually than simply seeing the power of God. Toward the end of the book of Exodus (33:12-23) we find Moses on Mount Sinai talking with God. It was the third time he had climbed this mountain, and it had become his place of meeting with God. He had just come through a very emotionally draining time. The last time he had descended from the mountain he found his people worshiping an idol, a golden calf, having turned their backs on the one true God. In his fury Moses threw down and broke the stone tablets bearing the Ten Commandments that God had given him. Now at this third time on the mountain, God encouraged him to continue to lead his people and even gave him a hopeful glimpse of the future.

Moses then requested two things from God. First, he needed confirmation once again that God's presence would be with him. In the past merely God's assurance of this had been enough for Moses to proceed. When at the burning bush he had felt inadequate to go and lead his people out of Egypt, it was God's guarantee of his presence that gave Moses the courage to accept the challenge. This time, however, Moses needed something more in order to go on. And he therefore made a second request. "Show me your glory," he asked God. In other words, he asked to see God's face, to see him in his full majesty, in all his splendor.

Moses' desire to see God in his full glory simply means seeing God as he truly is: that he is indefinable, mysterious, beyond anything we can grasp.

Russian Christians delight in the mystery of God, in the thought that we cannot know everything. They actually find security in this, because to them it truly guarantees that it is God whom they are worshiping—one so great that he is actually unfathomable. We in the West, however, are usually quite the opposite: we expect to understand the mysteries and seek to rid Christianity and God of the unknown.

In an Orthodox church there is a tall, decorated partition that completely separates the altar from the area for worshipers. It is usually covered with beautifully painted icons and often with gold leaf. This partition is called the iconostasis, and it symbolizes a fundamental emphasis of the Russian Orthodox Church—the mystery at the heart of the worshiper's adoration for God. The point of the iconostasis is that God cannot be encircled by our dogma and doctrine. God goes beyond the limits of what we as humans can know, much less define and articulate. So the other side of the iconostasis, the hidden area we cannot see, symbolizes a God beyond all our imaginings. And the worshipers stand in front, in shadowy candle-light, pondering this mystery at the heart of their worship.

In every Orthodox service the priest sings or says the following prayer, which is called "The Thrice-Holy Hymn":

> It is fitting and right to sing to you, to bless you, to praise you, to give thanks to you, to worship you in every place of your dimension: for you are God, beyond description, beyond understanding, invisible, incomprehensible, always existing, always the same; you and your only-begotten Son and your Holy Spirit.[2]

I find the fourth chapter of Revelation one of my favorite passages in the Bible. It describes John's vision of *the throne in Heaven.* It depicts some very unusual images—such as twenty-four elders, dressed in white and wearing gold crowns, surrounding God's throne. Four creatures resembling a lion, an ox, a man and a flying eagle, all with six wings and covered with eyes, continuously sing day and night, "Holy, holy, holy is the Lord God Almighty, who was, and is, and is to come" (v. 8). Whenever these four creatures give glory, honor and thanks to God, the twenty-four elders bow down before God and lay their crowns before him saying, "You are worthy, our Lord and God, to receive glory and honor and power, for you created all things" (v. 11).

Many people from scholars to artists have tried to explain Revelation 4 or to illustrate what each unusual figure represents and symbolizes. Often the many conclusions contradict each other. But I believe that the greatest message of this passage is simply that God is totally other, indescribable, beyond our comprehension—holy, majestic and awesome. This echoes the apostle Paul's words when he says: "No eye has seen, no ear heard, or mind has conceived, what God has prepared for those who love him" (1 Cor 2:9).

The exterior architecture and interior design of cathedrals throughout the former Soviet Union express the majesty and mystery of God. In the center of St. Petersburg stands St. Isaac's Cathedral, one of the most beautiful places of worship in the world, with beautiful golden domes—and to anyone with any imagination, the wonder of the place speaks for itself. During the Soviet era there hung from the large central dome in the middle of the church a huge pendulum that swung back and forth. During that time the church was a museum, and the communists had put the pendulum there to signify that they had scientifically explained away God. So often we also in a symbolic sense hang pendulums, explaining away the unknowns about God. As a result our Christian faith can become commonplace, even trivial.

Nowhere in the former Soviet Union did I experience more intensely this mystery and majesty of God than in the city of Tbilisi, Georgia, in the Caucasus Mountains. On several occasions I visited the patriarch of the Georgian Orthodox Church, Ilya II, and I took every opportunity to attend services at the historic Sioni Cathedral in the heart of the city. Ancient ceiling frescoes, colorful wall murals, hundreds of candles, royal vestments, brass- and gold-embossed Bibles and beautiful a cappella music all led me to feel very close to God while at the same time sensing his mystery as never before.

The Georgian church has a special appreciation for St. John Chrysostom, archbishop of Constantinople in the early fifth century, who was exiled by Emperor Arcadius to Transcaucasia. He died in 407 on his journey to a remote Georgian village on the eastern shore of the Black Sea. One of his most famous treatises was "The Unknowability of God." He emphasized in his preaching that God is a mystery beyond our understanding. Although God is near, closer to us than our own hearts, he always remains one who is beyond and above all that we know. Chrysostom encouraged his followers not to try to make God fit their reason.

Most of the magnificent cathedrals in Eastern and Western Europe were built during a period of Christianity that emphasized the mystery and majesty of God. This is still true of the few contemporary cathedrals even outside the European context. I remember reading an article about French architect Pierre Fakhoury, who built the Cathedral of Nôtre Dame de la Paix in Côte d'Ivoire, West Africa, where I once attended secondary school. This cathedral, completed in the early 1990s in the city of Yamoussoukro, is the largest basilica in the world today. It truly is breathtaking to see or—more accurately—to experience. Fakhoury said that while building this spectacular cathedral, "I had a strong feeling of terror at the thought of housing God. The terror comes from the realization that it is God; the one, the only, the great, the finest and the strongest."

The most famous cathedral in Russia is St. Basil's in Red Square. It has been called the most photographed building in the world—an extraordinary agglomeration of a dozen completely unmatched domes and spires in a multitude of colors, shapes and sizes. The best word to describe it is indefinable: your eyes strain to grasp it; your mind stretches to define it. Each step to your right or left makes the cathedral look significantly different because of the magical variety of domes. The story is told that between 1555 and 1561 Czar Ivan ("the Terrible") commissioned two architects, Barma and Postnik, to build a cathedral next to the Russian seat of power—a cathedral to honor God and to remind the people that God had delivered the Russian state from Mongol domination. The architects ended up building the extraordinary Cathedral of St. Basil. Czar Ivan was so awestruck by its beauty that he ordered the architects' eyes to be put out so that no one could ever again create such a building. How like this cathedral God is! Just when we think we have grasped him in our vision, a move one or two degrees spiritually to one side or the other presents us with a very different picture of who God is and what he is like.

Several times before his third trip up Mount Sinai, Moses had received a glimpse of the majesty of God. Just after God had miraculously parted the Red Sea, creating an escape route for his people, it is recorded that Moses sang a song. This "Song of Moses" repeatedly emphasizes the majesty of God: "Who among the gods is like you, O LORD? Who is like you—majestic in holiness, awesome in glory, working wonders?" (Ex 15:11).

This third time on Mount Sinai, however, he requested a more permanent view of God's glory, of his majesty and splendor. In response God allowed him to see his back. When Moses descended from the mountain, his face was radiant. He actually had to wear a veil as the radiance was too blinding, too terrifying for the people. In seeing God's glory Moses received what he needed spiritually—assurance to continue his walk with God and his hard task of leading the people to the Promised Land.

Russian Orthodox seminarians often study Western literature such as Shakespeare's plays. Once a Russian theological student reminded me of that marvelous passage at the end of Shakespeare's *King Lear:* "We too will away to prison—and laugh at the world—and take upon us the mystery of things as if we were God's spies." Only in seeing God's majesty and mystery can we gain and maintain that sense of awe of God that we desperately need. And the most appropriate reaction in the face of such mysteries is worship—because seeing God in his glory and majesty shines light on who we are and what we are like.

Humility and Worship—Our Sole Response

Another central emphasis of Russian Christians is their humility as God's children. The interior design of all Russian Orthodox churches is very similar—it is a design that symbolizes the humility of the worshipers as well as the otherness of God. An Orthodox church has four levels. The highest level is the ceiling, or the inside of the largest dome. Here there is a painting or fresco of Christ or an illustration representing God the Father. On the next level down, which is usually just below the dome, the twelve apostles are depicted around the church. On the walls surrounding the interior of the church is the third level, which is used to illustrate Russian saints, faithful Christian men and women throughout the centuries. The fourth level is simply the floor, where the people stand to worship today. Often the design of the church's exterior also denotes a Christian's humble position before God. This is illustrated in Kiev's finest architectural legacy, the eleventh-century Cathedral of St. Sophia, modeled after St. Sophia's in Constantinople. It has thirteen golden domes, one much larger and higher that represents Christ, and twelve smaller domes that are dramatically lower and represent the twelve apostles.

I have sensed the majesty and mystery of God in the worship of the Georgian Orthodox Church as in no other place. Yet in the midst of all the emphasis on God's majesty, I have also sensed a profound humility. This could well stem directly from the origin of Christianity in that country. It is said that in the second century King Mirian of Georgia was converted to Christianity by a simple slave girl named Nina, from the Georgian colony of Cappadocia. Eventually the whole country officially adopted the faith around 330. A cross made from a vine, said to have been brought to Georgia by Nina, is preserved today in Sioni Cathedral in Tbilisi. This historic cross, which I have seen several times, is different from other crosses in that both sides of the horizontal beam actually point downward at 45° angles; it is a cross of submission. This cross is a unique reminder to the Georgian people of the origin of their faith—that Christ was brought to them by a humble slave girl.

An experience of mine in South Asia powerfully illustrates the response of humble worship when confronted with God's majesty. I had the privilege of participating in a unique private meeting with just over twenty individuals from another religious faith. I was the only Westerner there. These people had been studying the Christian faith on their own for quite a long time and were at this meeting to inquire still further. During the course of the evening I was asked to share in simple terms through a translator the central themes of Christianity. It was one of those occasions when you feel that something beyond the natural is taking place. As we shared about our faith, many of the listeners seemed very much in agreement with all we were saying. It was as if their personal faith-journeys had already brought them to Christian belief. At the end of the meeting we invited anyone wanting to talk in greater detail to stay behind—and twelve people did just that. They ranged from an elderly man of seventy to a young woman in her twenties. As we shared more about the meaning of becoming a Christian, it was obvious that we were talking to people who had already made up their minds. When we asked them if they wanted to pray to God expressing their belief in Jesus Christ and their desire to follow him, all twelve responded positively.

At this point we were all sitting on chairs in a semicircle, and I felt it would be best to pray with each person individually. I moved closer to the young man at the end of the semicircle. As soon as I closed my eyes to pray, I heard him get off the chair and push it away. Opening my eyes, I saw that he had prostrated himself on the ground face down and was crying and talking to God. I did likewise, and we prayed together. The second person did the same, positioning himself flat on the floor face down. So did the third, and the fourth. Each of the twelve in turn prostrated themselves in order to pray. I had a very strong feeling that they realized that this was not just another god to whom they were speaking but the true God. And as a result they saw themselves for who they really were, and the only adequate response was to prostrate themselves in front of him.

In order to see God's glory, to have that renewed perspective of awe for God and consequently a sense of our own humble state, we need to ask him to keep on putting an end to our selfish desires, replacing them with his glory. This mirrors the apostle Paul's thoughts when he wrote those well-known words, "I no longer live, but Christ lives in me" (Gal 2:20).

I found the believers in the former Soviet Union very challenging in their humility. They have come through so much suffering: prisons, labor camps, harassment of all kinds, family separations, economic hardships and so on. You sense their deep belief that it is only God's Spirit dwelling in them that gives their lives meaning and value. I will never forget attending a small Baptist church in a converted country house on the outskirts of Moscow. To this day it remains one of my most profound experiences of Russia. As the snow fell outside, we huddled tightly together in a small, very overcrowded room. The service lasted for several hours and consisted mostly of prayers of thanksgiving and singing accompanied by an old pump organ. Most of the people were quite elderly. It was a service full of paradox. The worshipers were very serious, but the atmosphere was one of deep joy and gratitude.

It was not until communion time, toward the end of the service, that I clearly understood my feelings. Drinking from the cup and passing it to the elderly lady next to me, I watched as it moved from hand to hand around the room and was suddenly struck by the realization that these were people who had suffered deeply as I had never known suffering. The wrinkles in their faces, the gentleness of their penetrating and often tearful eyes, and the sweetness of their smiles said it all. And it was most obvious that it was their suffering that enabled them to sing as no other people could sing, out of their life experiences, of the greatness of God.

Moses, standing on Mount Sinai, asked to see God's glory. God responded by saying, "You cannot see my face, for no one may see me and live" (Ex 33:20). In a very real sense Moses was asking God for too much. He would have to die in order to see God fully. The

Bible says that when the Lord passed in front of Moses and showed him only his back, Moses' response was to fall immediately to the ground and worship him.

This was something with which Moses was familiar. When God appeared to him through a burning bush, he had to hide his face, for he was afraid to look at God. On another occasion, when God was to be present on Mount Sinai, he ordered Moses to put a boundary limit around the foot of the mountain to keep the people a safe distance away from him. If they crossed the limit, they would be too close to God and would die. This is a common theme throughout the Bible. The book of Revelation mentions that John was taken up and given a vision of God. John then says, "When I saw him, I fell at his feet as though dead" (Rev 1:17).

God showed his glory to Moses because of Moses' humility and his willingness to die to his own self. There was a time in his life when his assistants, his sister Miriam and brother Aaron, wanted more leadership power. They did not want God to speak to the people only through Moses but also through them. Numbers 12:3 then tells us in parenthesis, "(Now Moses was a very humble man, more humble than anyone else on the face of the earth.)" The passage continues with God saying: "When a prophet of the LORD is among you, I reveal myself to him in visions, I speak to him in dreams. But this is not true of my servant Moses. . . . With him I speak face to face, clearly and not in riddles; he sees the form of the LORD" (Num 12:6-8). Moses was clearly an exception because of his humility.

During the Soviet era many seminaries that were able to receive Western theological and philosophical literature obtained them mainly from France, where dissident Russians and anti-Soviet supporters had secret printing presses for like-minded individuals in the Soviet Union. Consequently, Blaise Pascal's writings are very familiar to and popular with Russian Orthodox priests. Pascal says in his

Pensées, describing the mystery and majesty of God in relation to man's humility:

> If there were no obscurity man would not feel his corruption; if there were no light man could not hope for a cure. Thus it is not only right but useful for us that God should be partly concealed and partly revealed, since it is equally dangerous for man to know God, without knowing his own wretchedness, as to know his wretchedness without knowing God.

I remember the privilege of visiting the Sussex home of Malcolm Muggeridge, author, journalist and broadcaster, in 1987, shortly before he died. He had been significantly influenced by the spirituality of the Russians, as his autobiographical writings show. In speaking about the mystery and majesty of God, he once said, "I believe worship should belong to the mystery, rather than what so many people are trying to make it, an extension of everyday life."[3] In his writings he tells of an occasion when he attended a service in a crowded Kiev church on a Sunday morning, when he was very moved at the depth of worship. "Never before or since have I participated in such worship," he recorded, feeling as a result closer to God than ever before. He felt the worshipers were turning to God with "a humility impossible to convey" and found no other recourse than to throw themselves on God's mercy.[4]

Saying goodbye that afternoon to Malcolm Muggeridge, I said, "I guess we may not meet again—but I'll see you in heaven." I will never forget his response. He put his hand on my shoulder with great seriousness and said, "Oh, I don't really know about that."

I left his house that day somewhat perplexed. Here was someone who had greatly influenced my personal Christian pilgrimage, who often spoke and wrote of looking forward to heaven, and yet he had just seemed to express his lack of assurance in ever getting there. A former theology professor of mine who knew Malcolm well was with me that day. He told me that Malcolm did not necessarily have doubts about his eternal destiny, but rather he had a very high view of heaven, seeing it as a precious and undeserved gift from God, certainly not something to mention casually.

The only prerequisite for seeing God in his full glory is seeing ourselves as we really are. And there is only one response to seeing his majesty, and that is falling down on our faces in worship.

Scripture's last words about the life of Moses are found at the end of Deuteronomy. After the description of his death it goes on to say:

> Since then, no prophet has risen in Israel like Moses, whom the LORD knew face to face, who did all those miraculous signs and wonders the LORD sent him to do. . . . For no one has ever shown the mighty power or performed the awesome deeds that Moses did in the sight of all Israel. (Deut 34:10-12)

The lives and experiences of Christians throughout the former Soviet Union and Eastern Europe require us to ask ourselves if we still stand in awe of God, conscious of our humble state. Whatever stage we have reached in our Christian pilgrimage, these Christians encourage us to have as our prayer the request of Moses: "LORD, show me your glory."

Praises of the Most High
You alone are holy, Lord God, wonder of wonders.
You are strong.
You are great.
You are the Most High.
You are omnipotent, Our Holy Father, Lord of Heaven and earth.
You, Lord God, one and three, are our every good.
You, Lord God, are good, our highest good—
 Lord God living and true.
You are charity and love.
You are wisdom.
You are humility.
You are patience.
You are a firm anchor.

You are peace.

You are joy and happiness.

You are justice and temperance.

You are full of riches.

You are beauty.

You are gentleness.

You are our protector.

You are our guardian and defender.

You are our strength.

You are our refreshment.

You are our great hope.

You are our faith.

You are our most profound sweetness.

You are our eternal life, great and admirable Lord,

Omnipotent God, Holy and Merciful Saviour.

A prayer of Saint Francis of Assisi

—2—

Keep On
Keeping On

From the Forgotten Faithful in the Middle East

Images of the Middle East in the Western media tend to be very* serious—wars, bombings, kidnappings, terrorism, Muslim fundamentalism, dictatorships, religious persecution, human rights abuse and so on. This uncivilized depiction may well be the only perspective that many in the West have of the cradle of civilization. One aspect of the Middle East that is almost always lost in its Western portrayal is humor. As perhaps nowhere else in the world, humor is a key characteristic of this region—as anyone who has lived there would confirm. Each person would have a wealth of diverse stories that would bring great laughter in their telling.

For example, Golda Meir, the former Israeli prime minister, once said, "Moses led our people all over the Middle East and settled on the only real estate without oil." And once, on a flight across the Red Sea from Jeddah (in Muslim Saudi Arabia) to East Africa, I sat near an Arab woman covered in the traditional black Islamic women's dress. Only her eyes remained unveiled, and I began to pity her for having to dress like that in the horrific heat. After all, we were heading for Djibouti, said to be the hottest country in the world. Once in the air when the seat belt light switched off, she stood up and walked to the toilet at the rear of the plane. A few minutes later she strolled back down the aisle not only unveiled, but dressed in what looked like Parisian haute couture, straight out of *Vogue* or *Elle* magazine.

The Middle East is a region of paradox. For example, I remember being in a hotel in a Muslim Arab country where it was illegal to be a Christian and where a fundamentalist Muslim man, with a full beard and dressed in a white cap and robe, tapped his foot and mouthed the words to the song he did not understand that was being played in the hotel lobby. This song was none other than "The Hallelujah Chorus" from Handel's *Messiah:* "The Kingdom of our Lord and of His Christ . . . Hallelujah."

The Middle East can be a very confusing place, and as a result Westerners often choose not to pay it much attention. To many it has become a terra incognita. More specifically, Christians in the Middle East are to many the most unknown entity. Some are even surprised to learn that not only does Christianity continue to exist but it even flourishes in parts of the Middle East. Christianity in the Middle East is largely an Arab Christianity. And for too many Christians in the West the Arab Christians are forgotten.

Our Middle Eastern Roots

It is so easy for us to forget that the Christian faith, our faith, comes from the Middle East. What we consider to be *our* Christianity originated as a Middle Eastern faith—but tragically, many churches in the West today think about the region no more than twice a year, at Christmas and Easter.

It is very interesting to see how the Bible includes the whole Middle East in God's redemptive plan—not just Palestine—and this is clear from the outset of the covenant stories in Genesis 12, 15, 17 and beyond. If Abraham were alive today, he would be considered an Iraqi because he comes from Haran, a place not far from modern-day Basra, near the Iraq-Kuwait border. The Persians lived in the country that is today Iran, and the prophet Daniel served faithfully in Babylon, just eighty miles south of Baghdad, Iraq's capital city. Two books of the Bible are set in what is today Iran—Nehemiah (named after the man who engineered the architectural plan for the city of Jerusalem) and Esther (which tells the story of a Jewish girl who won a Persian beauty contest). The greatest revival before Pentecost took place in Nineveh, the capital of what was then Assyria and is now Iraq. In the whole of the Old Testament we see God's love in a choreography that brought the whole Middle East together. In the New Testament story of Jesus' birth we read that Eastern astrologers came to the manger—the wise men were probably from Iraq. And baby Jesus ended up being a Palestinian refugee in Egypt.

Today it is easy to overlook the fact that most Christians in the Middle East are members of churches whose roots go back to Jesus' ministry, to Pentecost and to the witness of the early church. In the second chapter of Acts we read how the church was born: among those present in Jerusalem at the time were Arabs, Egyptians, Libyans, Medes and residents of Mesopotamia (Acts 2:9-10). These are all peoples of the Middle East today. The disciples in the upper room spoke Aramaic—a language that is related to Arabic. These Pentecost leaders returned to their homes as missionaries throughout the Middle East. Mark is believed to have taken Christianity to Egypt; Matthew to Ethiopia; Thomas to India and central Asia; Paul and Peter to Italy, Greece and Turkey; and Bartholomew to Armenia. Today's Arab Christians are the direct descendants of these Pentecost Christians.

Many Christians in the West are under the impression that believ-

ers in the modern-day Middle East are the result of Western missionary work in the last century. I remember hearing someone ask,
"When did the Palestinian Christians convert to Christianity?"—a
similar question to "Do the Russians use the Russian King James
Bible?" (as I was once asked). This is quite a misunderstanding of
history! In Western theological colleges the study of church history
begins in Jerusalem and proceeds quickly westward with the apostle
Paul. Then there is a jump from the early church fathers to the medi-
eval Roman Catholic Church and the Protestant Reformation. Consequently, a student can be left with the impression that the church
somehow ceased to exist in the lands of its origin. This is often erro-
neously attributed to the rise of Islam in the seventh century, on the
false assumption that Muslims put an end to Christianity in the Middle East.

It is no surprise, then, to see the astonishment of Western believers who learn that 15 percent of the Palestine Liberation Organization (PLO) are Christians. The Palestinian president, Yasir Arafat,
has now invited Western churches to come and minister in the West
Bank and Gaza. His wife, Soha Arafat, is a practicing Greek Orthodox Christian—and very proud of her heritage. Many Westerners are
equally surprised to discover that it was the Assyrian Church (in
Baghdad) that was the first to commission missionaries to China.
That happened in A.D. 415.

It is vital for us to realize and remember that our Christianity is
Middle Eastern in origin. Otherwise we lose the true identity of our
faith, which can make a significant difference to our Christian faith
and growth. Most of us have heard people newly returned from visiting Israel say how much it has enhanced their reading of the Bible.
They have now experienced the sights, sounds and smells of the
Bible and can picture the events in their contexts. This prison of for-
getfulness deprives us from learning from the rich Christian faith
and experience of the Middle Eastern Christians whose ancestors

founded the very faith that has changed our lives and that we now call our own.

Forgotten but Faithful

Despite being forgotten, Christians in the Middle East have been profoundly faithful. They have carried on an unbroken witness to the Christian faith—often under intense persecution—since the day of Pentecost. Throughout the centuries God's people have remained in those Middle Eastern cities, enduring sporadic outbursts of violent persecution and lingering oppression from many sources. The churches in the Middle East have a history of repeated harassment: the Byzantine Empire's oppression of Egyptian Christians for centuries; four hundred years of Turkish oppression, including the Turkish holocaust of Armenian Christians; Persian invasions between the fourth and sixth centuries; the Muslim Ottoman Empire; crusades by Western Christians, such as the sacking of Constantinople in 1204, colonialist exploitation by the French and British, and Western control of oil and natural resources; nationalist movements among Arab, Kurdish, Turkish and Jewish peoples; and oppression by the majority religion today—Islam.

The Oriental Orthodox Church, for example, has been among the most harassed and persecuted. There were times when three to four hundred thousand Christians were killed annually by Mogul emperors and their invading armies. The Assyrian Church, one of the oldest churches of the East, has never been able to settle in one specific country. Because of persecution and massacres its believers were forced to emigrate every hundred years or so. Many times it has lost all its possessions, including church buildings, schools and theological institutions, and has given up many martyrs—murdered because of their faith.

According to tradition the early church began in times of harsh persecution, with eleven of Jesus' twelve disciples having been martyred. From A.D. 67 to 303 there were ten significant outbreaks of persecution against Christians. And in varying forms it continues today. It is therefore no surprise that the rich tradition of Middle Eastern Christianity teaches much about martyrdom. For centuries Christians have been deeply wounded and their faith kept alive under tremendous pressure. They have endured much, and yet they are still present there, more than twelve million Christians in ancient and modern churches, carrying out powerful ministries in the midst of some of the most difficult circumstances on earth.

Keep On Keeping On—Perseverance

If there is one thing that stands above all else about these forgotten Christians, it is their perseverance. They keep on keeping on and have much to teach us about persevering and enduring in the midst of life's difficulties.

In the West we do not use the words "perseverance," "endurance" or "persistence" often in our Christian vocabulary. William Bennett, former United States Secretary of Education, wrote a bestseller, *The Book of Virtues*—in which the longest chapter is about perseverance. Yet perseverance remains one of the least romantic of virtues in Western Christianity. We often prefer to focus on seeing something take place immediately, looking for victory, a way out, healing or recovery. All of these have elements of truth in them. But I have been amazed to see how often the words "persevere," "endure" or "persist" occur in Scripture. Hebrews 12, for example, is essentially about perseverance. To the Middle Eastern reader of that day Hebrews 12 would immediately have brought to mind an athletic contest. The passage begins: "Since we are surrounded by such a great cloud of witnesses . . . let us run with perseverance the race marked out for us" (v.1)—suggesting an athletic event in a great arena or stadium. The spectators are the "cloud of witnesses," referring to an extensive list of individuals presented in chapter 11 as heroes of the faith. These heroes were Middle Eastern believers, men and women who persevered through some of the most hellish of situations and who are presented in Hebrews as inspiring examples to the believers of the first-century church. Equally today, Middle Eastern Christians continue to serve as an inspiration to us to keep on keeping on, no matter what difficulties or situations confront us.

The beginning of this famous Hebrews passage indicates in the words "the race marked out for us" that somehow each of us has a different race to run—and that we do not have the choice about which event we enter. A number of times in my life I have been in situations where I found myself very discouraged. In the midst of everything feeling so wrong there was a much deeper sense that it was right. The whole of Hebrews 12 pictures the Christian life as a long-distance race or long tournament, and not as a sprint or short match. And the word used for "perseverance" in the original language of these verses (Greek *hypomonē*) is related to "endurance," implying a discipline of strict training. It means a patience that masters things, not a patience that sits down and accepts things. After all, what athlete could ever win without determination? The writer of Hebrews is saying that whatever the obstacles or discouragement, we should not be stopped. We should not give up too quickly or collapse until the finish line is passed. It is an invitation to carry on to the end.

The ancient Greek games, the origin of our modern Olympic Games, were played in the cities of Delphi, Nemea, Olympia and Poseidon. At the beginning of the games each athlete, covered from head to toe with gold dust, came into the arena and stood with his father or trainer before a huge statue of the god Zeus, who had two thunderbolts in his hands. To Zeus he would make three vows; first, he had trained for ten months (discipline); second, he would compete according to the rules (fairness); and third, he would endure (perseverance). It is to these three vows that the writer of Hebrews is referring when he gives his encouragement to persevere.

For us to persevere in each of our own "races" we need to keep our eyes on the finish line; we must be farsighted, keeping the end in view. In any contest an eye for the finish line is absolutely essential, and the author of Hebrews turns this analogy into a means of focusing on Jesus. He says, "Let us fix our eyes on Jesus, the author and perfecter [or finisher] of our faith [the race]" (12:2).

Athletes must keep the final reward in view as an inspiration and encouragement to persevere in what is at times grueling training. In this way their toil, sweat, tears, and sufferings are balanced out with the rewards of victory—the sense of personal achievement, a trophy or gold medal, recognition and fame. I have always found it fascinating to see the winner of a long-distance race stumble across the finish line, collapse from exhaustion and dehydration, and then stand up and run the victory lap seemingly effortlessly with a smile as he or she waves to the crowds.

It is this reward for finishing that the author of Hebrews refers to in using Jesus as an example, saying that as a result of finishing his work he "sat down at the right hand of the throne of God" (12:2). Now the finish line for our race as Christians is Jesus himself. For many evangelical Christians in the West the study of Jesus and the Gospels does not play as significant a role in the growth of their faith as do the epistles of Paul. Christians in the Middle East tend to focus more on Jesus and his life. After all, he is their compatriot as far as they are concerned. We in the West should give more attention to Jesus, since the primary goal of the Christian life is Christlikeness. In this sense, no matter what type of race our Christian life seems to be—a marathon, the hurdles or an obstacle course—it is a race heading toward a clear finish line.

With this clear goal before us, our Christian lives should be active and dynamic, full of a sense of purpose and direction. In this sense we could be contrasted with tourists visiting the Middle East. It is very easy in Middle Eastern medinas (the old city districts) to determine whether someone is a tourist or a resident. The tourists are always stopping, trying to find road signs down the ancient, winding alleys. In contrast a resident walks with an obvious air of confidence as to where he or she is going. Ours is not a "touristic" faith. Instead it is a faith with a clear sense of direction toward attaining the likeness of Christ.

The writer of Hebrews relates perseverance to discipline and training. In Western culture we often associate the word "discipline" with some form of punishment. Yet in Hebrews discipline is cast in a very different light, as a *positive* rather than a *negative* word. This spiritual discipline is a facilitator and contributor toward Christian growth. It matures us in our Christian walk, enables us to see God at work in different ways, refines us and develops our spiritual life by stretching our faith's boundaries. With this perspective difficulties and suffering end up serving as the training ground for spiritual growth.

When I was in secondary school, I played on the school basketball team. One year we had a winning season that took us to the regional championship game. I can well remember a running exercise our coach put us through in preparation for that championship game. This exercise was grueling, and we called it a "monster." It made us dread going to the practice sessions. Yet in the championship game itself, there is no question that the conditioning we had undergone enabled us to win. We ended up grateful for having had to tackle those "monsters."

For whatever reasons (and many we do not and will not totally understand), the difficult times of our lives are used to bring greater depth into our Christian life. Suffering is one of the paradoxes of Christian truth. Paradox can often be one of the most effective and authentic means of communicating and introducing truth. This is why theological communicators such as Søren Kierkegaard, Karl Barth and Reinhold Niebuhr used paradox so often. The Scriptures are full of paradox, indicating that God often communicates with us this way. Suffering is an example of paradox: at one level it tears down, yet at a deeper level it builds up. So paradoxically we gain through the losses. And such is the case with Christians during this intermission of eternity that we call life.

When living in Carthage in Tunisia (an Arab Muslim country) I was told the story of an event in the life of Hannibal, the Carthaginian general. He had successfully routed the Roman legions, though the odds had been stacked against him. When winter came he wintered his troops in Capua, a city he had captured. Capua was considered a city of luxury, and one winter in Capua did what the Roman legions had not succeeded in doing. The luxury and ease so sapped the morale of the Carthaginian troops that when the spring came and the campaign was resumed, they were unable to stand before the Romans. Ease had ruined them where struggle had bettered them.

Having to persevere during the difficulties that come our way can often seem unfair or disillusioning. Yet at the same time this perseverance can end up as instructive training at the deepest level of our spiritual development. This echoes what James, who was himself persecuted and martyred in the Middle East, says in his well-known words: "The testing of your faith develops perseverance. Perseverance must finish its work so that you may be mature, and complete, not lacking anything" (Jas 1:3-4).

The author of Hebrews goes on to say that the Lord "punishes" everyone he accepts as his child (Heb 12:6). The first-century Middle Eastern Christian would understand the word "punishes" as "whips." Again this whole passage continues to use the analogy of an athletic event. During the ancient Greek games when athletes stopped or lost their balance, they were beaten with rods to help them stay on track and motivate them to keep going. The athlete did not view such beatings adversely but rather saw them as offering help to finish and fulfill their vow, "I will endure." Ironically, with this interpretation, "punishment" becomes a positive word to the one being punished.

A few years after university I went through a very difficult time. I experienced much hurt and disillusionment brought on by a number of different circumstances during a period of about a year and a half. While the hurt left me feeling wounded, the disillusionment left me isolated from friends and the Christian community, the church. I would never want to experience another period like that again. As I look back on that time, however, there is no question that as a result of it I experienced and learned more from God than ever before in my life. Experiencing difficulties in life somehow enabled me to see the beauty of God. And the sweet is far stronger than the bitter. While not wanting to experience it again, paradoxically, I am grateful for it.

Christians in the Middle East are focused on the finish line, enabling them to endure and remain in the race despite all the suffering they have experienced. They live with daily conflicts of one sort or another. During a visit to Jerusalem I was struck by the realization that the front-page shootings and bomb threats I read about in *The Jerusalem Post* each morning were typical daily news events. The Christians in the Middle East believe that God has special plans for their part of the world, and they want to be of assistance. Despite the enormous pressures—both the psychological and social pressures of living as a minority community and the economic, religious and political pressures—thousands of Middle Eastern Christians are aware of their calling to a Christian presence and witness in these lands where Jesus and his disciples walked and taught.

I know of an evangelical Christian leader in Lebanon who decided to leave Beirut during the civil war to live in Europe. After all, it seemed logical. He had young children, and the danger could only escalate. Thousands of Lebanese had already emigrated to the stability of Europe or the United States. He and his wife sold their belongings, moved out of the house where they were living and made all the necessary arrangements to leave the country, including buying plane tickets. The departure date arrived, and he and his family, together with all they could stuff into suitcases, headed for the airport in south Beirut. As he was waiting to check in, both he and his wife felt unsettled and came to the conclusion that God was telling them to stay in Beirut and minister in the midst of the crisis; they were needed in Lebanon, not in Europe. They turned around and returned to their home. Over the years this man has served as one of the most significant catalysts in the church for healing and peace, working with the many church traditions in this war-torn country.

I have had the privilege of working with a number of Coptic Orthodox priests in Egypt who minister faithfully and dynamically in the midst of very difficult circumstances. They receive constant threats from the Islamic authorities. Some Christian churches have been burned to the ground by Muslim militants. Often the government does not allow them to repair their ancient church buildings, let alone build extensions to hold the ever-growing numbers of people attending their services. They even suffer ostracism and discouragement from their own denominational leaders who, attempting to be diplomatic in their relationship with the Muslim authorities, are afraid of being too closely identified with the expanding ministries of these priests. Despite these and many other restrictions and hardships they continue to serve faithfully, proactively and joyfully. As a result they are seeing God bless their ministries with many coming to an understanding of the Christian faith. On one moving occasion a friend of mine, a Coptic Orthodox priest, showed me where he had privately baptized five young men from a Muslim background the night before. He went on enthusiastically to recount the testimonies they had each given prior to baptism of how they came to the Christian faith. It was obvious that he lived for this purpose, at the risk of dying for it at the same time.

It was an unforgettable experience to meet Asma. She lives in an Arab Muslim country under *sharia,* Islamic law, whereby it is illegal to become a Christian. She grew up as the daughter of a respected *imam,* a Muslim cleric. He taught her the *Qur'an* (often called the Koran in the West) and even used her to teach others. In her study of the Qur'an she was struck by the mention of the cross and felt somehow that it held great significance. The Islamic teaching—that Jesus did not die but rather that someone else was put in his place—made no sense to her because it suggested that God was deceitful. This began her search for the truth of Christianity, and she began to observe the lifestyles of the few expatriate Christians in her country. She made her pilgrimage to Mecca, where she was shocked at the cruel way the Muslim nationals treated their foreign Asian servants, which seemed contrary to what she had been taught about Islam.

Her inner search for the truth eventually led her to the Christian faith. Her decision resulted in her husband divorcing her and her father taking away her children. She lost everything that was dear to her. However, she decided never to move to another country, despite having many opportunities to do so, believing that God wanted her to remain where she was. After a number of years she remarried and her new husband became a Christian. It was in this new context that she miraculously had the opportunity to be reunited with her children. She still faces ostracism and hostilities, yet she is committed to a Christian presence in this difficult country. She sat with me and joyfully told me story after story of what God is doing in her country in the midst of the hardships. I could not help but be reminded of the Christians in the early church.

It is no surprise then to see how much Middle Eastern Christians love the book of Revelation. They often quote from it. Throughout Revelation, the phrase "to him who overcomes" is used. At the end of the book when John writes about the New Jerusalem, we are told "He who overcomes will inherit all this" (Rev 21:7). In modern-day Turkey, the same country for which Revelation was originally written, Christians are still in very similar situations to those who first read those words.

The heart of Middle Eastern Christianity is revealed in its literature. It is here that we can most clearly understand the perspective on the pain and adversity that Christians have experienced. The following poem by Yusuf al-Khal, a Lebanese Christian poet, expresses perseverance in hardship through the figure of Jesus and his crucifixion.

> Thirsty? Take the rock and strike it.
> In the deep darkness? Roll it away from the tomb.
> Is it hunger that has seized you? Look, here is the manna
> And the quails. Are you brought to nakedness?
> Take fig leaves for a garment to cover
> Iniquity and hide it from men.
> In the great temptation have the patience
> Of Job and do not despair of blatant evil:
> The Cross of God is reared on the hill of endless time.[1]

The Check-and-Balance of Perseverance

Middle Eastern Christians not only provide us with a beautiful example of perseverance in the sufferings and struggles of life but also show us the necessity of developing a check-and-balance attitude. It is so easy and natural to respond to life's difficulties with self-pity, focusing (often accurately) on the fact that we do not deserve it—"Why me?" Or we can quite easily become resentful either toward the party responsible for the suffering or toward God himself. At other times, rather than looking externally for something to blame, we may do the opposite, being unnecessarily hard on ourselves. Each of these quite natural responses tends to breed restlessness, bitterness and a lack of inner peace.

The writer of Hebrews addresses this natural response to situations that require perseverance. He says that discipline seems painful, but it produces "peace for those who have been trained by it" (Heb 12:11). In other words, those who learn perseverance can live in genuine peace. The writer goes on to encourage those in difficulty to "make every effort to live at peace with all. . . . See to it that no one misses the grace of God and that no bitter root grows up" (Heb 12:14-15). In essence he is saying that there needs to be a constant check-and-balance in our perseverance, to prevent either the growth of bitterness or the building of walls between ourselves and others or ourselves and God.

Instead we need to focus our efforts on an exceptional—and even supernatural—response that results in being at peace no matter what our situation. We must actively develop such a response, however, and this can be very difficult to achieve because bitterness or resentment toward someone who is wronging us can be an automatic reaction. The Middle Eastern writer encourages us to try to predispose ourselves positively toward the growth of others. As a result of such perseverance, our character should all the more assist, not hinder, the welfare of others.

Middle Eastern Christians are learning to live at peace in the midst of hostility and conflict, immense tension and suffering. They have more reasons than anyone to be resentful and bitter, yet on the whole they are not. In working with them I have discovered their love for and emphasis on Jesus' Sermon on the Mount, and "Blessed are the peacemakers" is their abiding verse of guidance and purpose. As the late King Hussein of Jordan, a Muslim, has said, "Christians are the glue in the Middle East."

I will never forget the time I spent with a Protestant pastor in Egypt. Leader of one of the largest churches, he is an expert on the doctrine and beliefs of Islam, the majority religion in his country. For years he has been summoned by the secret police for interrogation. This often happens at the most inconvenient times such as late at night or just before an international trip. Yet as he shared these frustrating occurrences, it was obvious how much he genuinely cared even for the police. He loves his interrogators and has sincerely befriended them. He knows them by name and is concerned about their families. He even knows the desserts they like and sometimes, when summoned to the police station, takes to them desserts that his wife has made. The police do not know how to handle his kindness. Most strikingly in the midst of—or perhaps as a result of—these difficulties, he is absolutely radiant and does not have an ounce of anger or bitterness within him.

One friend of mine, Ibrahim, is from an Arab Muslim country currently in deep unrest due to Islamic militant fundamentalism involving rampant terrorism and bombings. Ibrahim became a Christian while studying in Europe, where he could have gone on to have a successful career—which is what his parents would have preferred. Instead Ibrahim chose to return to his country to work at encouraging and teaching the few Christians there. One of his most significant contributions has been his translation of the Bible into a local language, a work that put his life at great risk. Everyone who meets Ibrahim speaks of his deep sensitivity and compassion toward others. He exudes generosity. The hardness of his living situation has, paradoxically, softened him, and it is because of this softness or tenderness that Ibrahim is one of the strongest Christian leaders in his part of the world.

Perhaps one of the most powerful examples of perseverance is the life of Elias Chacour, who has become a friend of our family. He is a Palestinian Melkite (Eastern rite) Catholic priest in Israel, who has been nominated several times for the Nobel Peace Prize for his work in uniting Israeli Jews, Christians, Muslims and Druze in Galilee. He knows what it means to suffer and persevere. After World War II when many Jews returned to Palestine, his family was thrown off the land that had been their home for many generations and separated from one another for a considerable period of time during the disturbances. They lost all they owned, and Elias was sent away to a boarding school for his safety. Yet throughout these difficulties his parents taught him not to be bitter or resentful and to love as the Bible describes. He eventually became a priest and went to work in the town of Ibillin in Galilee, a place of great tension and strife. Over time he saw the entire community miraculously change as he lived among them in love, treating them all equally. He currently builds schools, libraries, community centers and youth clubs throughout Israel's Galilee region, and he travels the world speaking about living at peace with yourself, with others and with God.

When you spend time with Abuna (Father) Chacour, you are left with the profound certainty that, more than anything, perseverance has marked his life in the midst of great difficulty and discouragement. You are also left with a clear realization that his first calling is to be a peacemaker in the fullest sense of the word. He has thousands in his area praying for peace. Abuna simply radiates peace and joy. Children are drawn to him. My daughter, who was two years old when she first met him, still remembers Abuna years later. Perhaps more than anything, the many hardships he has faced have formed him into a man of gentleness. Young and old, regardless of their religion or ethnic group, gravitate toward this gentle Palestinian priest from Galilee. His life is a contemporary echo of that other Galilean who went before him many years ago.

In his book *Justice and Only Justice* Naim Stifan Ateek, an Anglican priest at St. George's Cathedral in Jerusalem, gives this advice to his fellow oppressed Palestinians, advice that is excellent counsel for us Westerners as well:

> So I consider the challenge to my fellow Palestinians to be threefold: Keep struggling against hate and resentment. Always confess that the struggle goes on and the battle is not over. At times you will have the upper hand, at times you will feel beaten down. Although it is

extremely difficult, never let hatred completely overtake you. By the power of God the struggle will go on until the day comes when you begin to count more victories than defeats. Never stop trying to live the commandment of love and forgiveness. Do not dilute the strength of Jesus' message: do not shun it, do not dismiss it as unreal and impractical. Do not cut it to your size, trying to make it more applicable to real life in the world. Do not change it so that it will suit you. Keep it as it is, aspire to it, desire it, and work with God for its achievement. Remember that so often it is those who have suffered most at the hands of others who are capable of offering forgiveness and love.[2]

If we find ourselves in the midst of persevering in life's struggles, we need to check continually to see if we have developed any resentment or bitterness. This check-and-balance leads us toward inner peace at the deepest level and a profound experience of the sweetness of the Christian life. The challenge from Middle Eastern Christians and the Scriptures is to keep on keeping on, to persevere through whatever we are facing or will face in the future. The greatest encouragement toward this end comes from the character of the Middle Eastern founder of our faith, our Lord Jesus Christ himself. Thanks to his love and faithfulness there is a sense of always knowing the final result of our efforts at perseverance. As James said, "As you know, we consider blessed those who have persevered. You have heard of Job's perseverance and have seen what the Lord finally brought about. The Lord is full of compassion and mercy" (Jas 5:11).

Perhaps no words are more powerful than those of an old Middle Eastern man in prison at the end of his life—a man who had suffered immeasurably during the giving of his life's service to promote the Christian faith. He wrote to a young timid man named Timothy who was just starting his ministry. This elderly Semitic man by the name of Paul said:

I have fought the good fight, I have finished the race, I have kept the faith. Now there is in store for me the crown of righteousness, which the Lord, the righteous Judge, will award to me on that day—and not only to me, but also to all who have longed for his appearing. (2 Tim 4:7-8)

Let us keep on keeping on.

A Muslim's First Prayer as a Christian
O God, I am Mustafah the tailor
and I work at the shop of Mohamed Ali.
The whole day long I sit
and pull the needle and the thread through the cloth.
O God, you are the needle
and I am the thread.
I am attached to you and I follow you.
When the thread tries to slip away from the needle
it becomes tangled and must be cut
so that it can be put back in the right place.
O God, help me to follow you
wherever you may lead me.
For I am only Mustafah the tailor,
and I work at the shop of Mohamed Ali
on the great square.[3]

Throughout this chapter, personal names have been changed and the names of countries withheld to protect the Middle Eastern Christians.

—3—

Celebrating Life

At Play in the Fields
of the Lord in Latin America

During a trip to Guatemala in Central America I had the opportunity of visiting a town by the name of Panajachel that sits on Lake Atitlán. It is one of the most beautiful and tranquil places I have ever seen. This little town—or, more accurately, village—sits beside the large fifty-square-mile lake that has three towering volcanoes rising along its shores. Between the volcanoes stand massive granite cliffs that beautifully reflect shades of gray, blue and purple, depending on the sun's position.

One morning just after dawn, with the sun still orange on the water, I arranged for a village man to take me out toward the middle of the lake in his motorboat. When we were a good distance from the shore, he cut the engine. The water was absolutely still, and we floated in silence, except for the splashes of occasional leaping fish. The sights, sounds and smells were enchanting. I experienced the deepest sense of calm and peace. And it was there, sitting on a boat in the middle of that lake, that the realization struck me: I was doing something I had not done for a long time—celebrating the gift of life. This so perfectly matched the Latin American culture surrounding me.

Christians in Latin America, most of whom are Hispanic, truly know how to celebrate life, and we have much to learn from them. European and American cultures emphasize comfort, entertainment and pleasure—yet celebrating life is not something at which we excel. We often hurry through life under pressure, too busy, feeling stress and tension. "Don't stop until you drop" is the motto of many who seem endlessly on the run. Consequently, we are familiar with words such as burnout, breakdown, exhaustion, fatigue, crisis and depression.

I once attended a Christian leadership conference in Holland where the workshop with the greatest attendance was entitled "Knowing Your Breaking Point." Recently a friend leading a large Christian ministry shared with me his concerns about becoming a workaholic. He had started to worry when he woke up one morning in his office chair, still dressed in his suit and tie, having thought that he had gone home the night before. He had lost touch with his life, let alone the ability to enjoy it.

Karl Barth, a renowned German theologian, once asked in a sermon on Psalm 111:10 the question, "What is wisdom?" He answered that it is knowing about life or the art of living. Norman Vincent Peale, a New York pastor, published his first book, *The Art of Living,* in 1937. It is still a bestseller today, indicating people's yearning to understand how to live life to the full.

Our lives are frequently so rushed that we do not stop to smell the flowers or allow our imaginations to flow, seeing shapes in the clouds. In our society it is all too easy to be so busy, even in doing good, that life just passes us by. We have all said or heard others say,

"I haven't had a real vacation for so long." Living God's gift of life to its fullest means allowing time for leisure and laughter—playing, relishing the moment and doing things for no reason other than just doing them. The artist Vincent van Gogh, whose passion for life is strikingly evident in his expressive paintings, said, "The best way to know life is to love many things."

It is interesting to recall our most vivid memories of childhood. Some of my best memories include the time my father attended my Sunday morning basketball game, skipping church to do so—and he was the pastor! Or the days when we went bird hunting together. Or when we visited Gambia in West Africa and stayed on the beach for several weeks, swimming during the day and playing board games at night. What will our children or grandchildren remember? As children, play comes naturally to us, but as we get older we often forget how to play.

Hispanics in both Central and South America vary in skin color, history, racial origins and sometimes in the ways they express their Christian faith. Their two central cultural characteristics are a marvelous sense of celebrating life through fiesta, resulting in a loving appreciation of God's gift of life, and an understanding of time that allows them to savor that gift. This is an explosive combination and a contagious one, holding a promise of much-needed vitality for us from other parts of the world. Every time I have visited Latin America I have come away with a renewed zeal for living. It has nothing to do with what people say; it is just who they are.

To many people, Latin America means drug cartels, illegal immigration, guerrilla activity, corrupt governments and squandered foreign investment. On the other hand, Latin America has a population of over 350 million people, an ever-increasing percentage of whom regard the Christian faith as the living option, a faith of true life. Consequently, the church is now one of the most important factors shaping human life and institutions throughout Latin America.

The Protestant churches are undergoing tremendous growth. The fastest-growing group in Latin America is the Pentecostals—approximately 75 percent of all Latin American Protestants belong to some Pentecostal or charismatic church. In many ways Christians have experienced a cultural liberation over the last thirty years, with their manner of worship coming to match their culture more closely. Consequently, much of the worship in churches—regardless of the denomination—is vigorous and lively, and it would be viewed by Western Christians as charismatic in style.

Many Hispanic Christians are discovering in this expression a living faith, in contrast to years of routine worship, ritual and an excessive traditionalism. The worst thing that can happen to these festive people is to become caged in rigid and overly structured worship in which they do not naturally feel comfortable. They flourish when allowed to act with great freedom. I once heard a Hispanic Christian describe his experience of worshiping for a significant period of time in a church of a different tradition from his own. It was a church recently begun and led by Westerners with a series of strict dos and don'ts and a lot of how-tos. He explained that he slowly began to lose his natural joy and optimism, and it was only on discovering a way of worshiping that was natural for him that his relationship with Jesus changed and his celebration of life returned.

While the church in Latin America is known for its vibrant life, ironically it is at the same time a suffering church. Latin American Christians have suffered ever since the Christian faith was brought to their continent. Christianity was introduced to Latin America by the Spanish and Portuguese conquerors at the turn of the fifteenth century. From the outset, therefore, Christian mission among the local people was politically related to both Christ and a European king.

Today the struggles continue in other ways. A French study prepared in 1979 for a conference of Christian clergy in Latin America held in Puebla, Mexico, recorded that 1,500 pastors, priests, nuns and lay Christians had endured arrest, interrogation, prison, torture and exile in recent years. Others had been anonymously executed and reported missing. Many Christians today live with constant instability and violence. Additionally, a great number of Christians are from the submerged class, thereby living within a culture of poverty.

They have suffered and continue to suffer greatly. They live under many daily limitations. Yet in the midst of their struggles, Latin American Christians possess the sterling quality of celebrating the gift of life in all its manifestations—joy and sorrow, pain and healing.

This quality in part results from their culture. When visiting Latin America you cannot help but observe the people's celebratory nature. I have not yet been able to fall asleep in a Latin American hotel, no matter how late it is, without the sound of dance music playing in the background. Somewhere in the neighborhood there is always a party going on late into the night.

Latin Americans have described themselves as having the following characteristics:

☐ easily carried away by emotions of compassion and tenderness

☐ known for their personal warmth, responsiveness and emotion

☐ hot-blooded, with passions running close to the surface

☐ optimistic and charged with a good sense of humor

Their art confirms this perspective on life. Ancient pre-Columbian sculptures depict humans not as freely walking or freestanding but rather restricted in projection by the surfaces of the architecture into whose block they are carved. Their cramped poses are in sharp contrast to the sensitive expressions on their faces. The image being communicated is that of a free spirit within a cramped situation. Another example is from the Mochica people in Peru, around A.D. 500, whose potters experimented with different types of facial expressions until they were able to produce natural, spontaneous and infectious ones—such as laughing individuals with wide, happy grins and eyes almost closed in laughter.

Today Latin American artistic creations—whether fabric designs, painting or pottery—are known for their spectacularly bright colors. Modern Latin American art is expressive. Whether an artist is a primitivist of Indian heritage or a modern abstract painter, he or she tends to work by catching your attention via the emotions.

The people of Latin America are also known for their joyous music. Music making envelops these people—using the marimba, harps, flutes, panpipes and drums, and the popular rhythms of calypso, salsa and samba. Dance is inherent to this musical culture, and we have all heard of the cha-cha, mambo, samba, tango and conga. The Latin American year is filled with holidays, and the annual calendar is guided by the many fiestas.

The Latin American approach to life is naturally one of celebration. When they find a deeper and more meaningful life in Jesus Christ, the people are truly able to celebrate life in its fullest dimension. As one Latin American Christian said, "It's just that we are a religious people, and spirituality flows in our veins."

The theme of celebrating life is seen throughout the Bible. In the creation story we are told that God worked and then he rested, communicating an active rather than a passive rest. In other words, he enjoyed his creation. The Scriptures go on to recount three different times when God himself laughed. We are also told that Moses and Abraham laughed. Throughout the Old Testament the words "joy," "gladness" and "celebrate" are synonymous for laughter. We read in Proverbs 17:22 that "a cheerful heart is good medicine."

The Westminster Shorter Catechism, written in 1647, begins with the words "Man's chief end is to glorify God and to enjoy him forever." This echoes the words of Augustine: "Love God and do what you please."

The Gospel of John is filled with the theme of life. John begins and ends his Gospel with an emphasis on life by writing of Jesus, "In him was life, and that life was the light of men" (Jn 1:4). At the very end we read that John's aim in writing was that "you may believe that Jesus is the Christ, the Son of God, and that by believing you may have life in his name" (Jn 20:31). The word "life" is continually on Jesus' lips and occurs more than fifty times throughout the Gospel in such well-known statements as "I am the bread of life," "The Spirit gives life," "Whoever believes in me, streams of living water will flow from within him," "I have come that they may have life to the full," "I have told you this . . . that your joy may be complete," "[You] will have the light of life," "I am the resurrection and the life."

John is attempting to communicate Jesus' message that there is a difference between existing and truly living. I was once sitting in a church that had on its eastern window the verse "I am the way and the truth and the life" (Jn 14:6), and I recall the contrast between the truth of that statement and the atmosphere and teaching of that church. There was nothing in the church service even to suggest to a visitor that the Christian faith was concerned with any sort of life at all.

The Gospel writer makes every attempt to present Jesus as a balanced person. We are told that Jesus took time to be by himself, that he had a good sense of humor, that he did not run through life but rather knew his mission clearly and refused to be rushed. Jesus had time for people—to talk to the Samaritan woman at the well, to comfort his disciples. He is even described enjoying a wedding party, sharing in the happy rejoicing of the event. He is never presented as serious, severe or an austere killjoy. It is interesting to note that it was at a village girl's wedding in a Galilean town that Jesus showed his divinity by performing his first miracle. This gives us an important glimpse into his personality and priorities.

All through the Bible we hear the echo of the message that in becoming Christians we enter a new kind of life. Following Jesus' way guarantees us his help for living, giving us a new sense of loveliness, a new attractiveness and a new strength. Our lives can become so lovely that we cannot conceive of anything more complete—other than heaven itself. As Christians we can be laughing pilgrims and disciples embracing life.

The Precious Present

One of the keys to the Latin American Christians' ability to celebrate life is that they live in the present. The American author Spencer Johnson wrote a bestselling book entitled *The Precious Present.* He tells the story of a little boy trying to discover the whereabouts of the precious present that an elderly man described to him. The profound message of the story is that the boy learns that the truly precious present is the ability to live in the present moment, relishing life in the now.

The Latin American mindset is concerned with the existential now. A cultural characteristic frequently attributed to Latin Americans is their understanding of time. They have been called a *mañana* (tomorrow) people. They are orientated to the present and have a tremendous ability to enjoy each moment to the full. Some Latin American Christians celebrate what they call "the sacrament of the present moment," taken from the work of the early eighteenth-century writer Jean-Pierre de Caussade. The thought behind it is that our lives are sacred; each present moment can be made a sacrament.

I have heard the story of some Westerners who were traveling through jungles such as the lush, dense, almost impenetrable forests of Amazonia. They had hired some local people to help them get through the jungle as quickly as possible, and they traveled for several days at a fast pace, covering a good distance. One day, as they prepared to set off on another day's traveling, they found their helpers sitting and resting and could not persuade them to get up. Confused, the Westerners asked for an explanation. The reply was that they needed to rest all day so that their souls could catch up with their bodies.

This ability to live in the present allows Christians in Latin America to relish God's gift of life. They meet their God in the present, and therefore their relationship to God is emotional, with a sense of urgency to it, connected to the immediate reality of life.

One Saturday afternoon found me shopping in the commercial Zona Rosa district of Mexico City. As I stood admiring a sculpture in a modern art shop, I was approached by an assistant who asked if she could help me. When I said how much I liked the sculpture, she used it as an illustration to share her Christian faith with me openly and ever so naturally. She put a particular emphasis on a recent experience of renewal that she had had. I must have stood in that shop in front of the sculpture listening and asking questions for three-quarters of an hour. She had such a fresh and contagious faith. To her, Christianity was definitely a life celebration.

Latin American Christians are keen to tell the tales of their experience of God. They are dynamic conversationalists, natural storytellers who relate their stories to the story of Jesus. I have rarely enjoyed church as much as I do in Cuba. Although the Cuban church has been worshiping under governmental restrictions for more than three decades, I have yet to find Christians anywhere with greater joy and hope. Their church services can be filled with more than two hours of music, singing and testimonies—so many stories about recent experiences of the faithfulness of God. It is a celebration of God's character from beginning to end.

Ecclesiastes—A Book About Living

Many view the book of Ecclesiastes as pessimistic, remembering the well-known refrain "all is meaningless." Others see it as an enigma, presenting both a pessimistic and optimistic view of life. However, the writer's aim is to defend faith in a generous, life-giving God by pointing to the meaninglessness and grimness of the alternative. This explains why the writer at times speaks of despair and gloom and at other times points us to the enjoyment of life. Throughout the book runs a thread of joy.

In the last part of chapter 2 and in chapter 3 of Ecclesiastes the writer considers the themes of enjoyment, beauty, God's gifts, security and joy. Through these he demonstrates that it is possible to receive the gift of enjoyment from the hand of God and consequently be able to revel in his creation. He says, "A man can do nothing better than to eat and drink and find satisfaction in his work. This too, I see, is from the hand of God" (Eccles 2:24). Here eating, drinking and work symbolize the totality of a joyful life. The writer is saying that the earthly realm and human endeavor are created inherently for enjoyment. God the Creator's fundamental mood is therefore one of joy, and his primary disposition toward us, his children, is one of giving.

However, the writer goes further by making the important observation that in the balance of life, laughter and dance go hand in hand with crying and mourning (Eccles 3:4). "[God] has made everything beautiful in its time" (Eccles 3:11), and during the various periods of life, in ease and hardship, in want or plenty, the enjoyment of God and his gifts remains a privilege he has given us. It is with this mindset that the author of Ecclesiastes wants the reader to approach life. God's intention for us, regardless of the days of darkness we experience, is to savor and enjoy his gift of life.

Central to Hispanic Christians' existence is this perspective that life is God's gift and that it is our duty to celebrate it with others. They will find any excuse to celebrate—birthdays, baptisms, weddings, funerals, even a meeting with friends can become a party. Any event is a potential fiesta. Hispanic Christians celebrate life in

all its manifestations—joy and sorrow, pain and healing, success and
failure, struggle and leisure, strength and weakness. Their view of
life echoes that held by the early nineteenth-century English artist
and poet William Blake, who experienced both profound states of
celebration and desperation throughout his life. In his poem "Augu-
ries of Innocence," he says:

> Man was made for Joy and Woe,
> And when this we rightly know,
> Thro' the World we safely go.
> Joy and Woe are woven fine.
> A Clothing for the Soul divine;
> Under every grief and pine
> Runs a joy with silken twine.[1]

The Old Man and the Sea, which earned Ernest Hemingway the
Pulitzer Prize and led to a Nobel Prize for Literature, is a short novel
mirroring the worldview that many Hispanic Christians hold. On
one level it is an exciting and tragic adventure story of an old Cuban
fisherman, Santiago, and a young Cuban boy, Manolin, and their
fishing exploits. On another level it is a religious parable, filled with
Christian symbols and metaphors. Santiago is seen as unvanquished,
with a noble acceptance of the limitations forced upon him. At its
deepest level the book is a fable of the unconquerable spirit of man,
capable of snatching spiritual victory from circumstances of disaster
and apparent defeat.

In states of desolation and consolation Hispanic Christians are
aware that God is always present. As feelings are so powerfully a
part of their lives, their natural disposition is to reflect continually on
the spiritual dimension: the Bible is proclaimed, prayed and sung as
a commentary on everyday life, while the experiences of everyday
life are told, prayed and sung as commentary on the Bible. In this
sense, they are much more interested in celebrating their experience
of God than theologizing about it.

I remember visiting a village on the border of the jungles of Petén in northern Guatemala. During an evening meal with a Christian Indian family I was told about an elderly man living in the village who had experienced great suffering recently and was believed to be dying. He had been the village lay pastor and was obviously highly respected. People were deeply concerned at the prospect of losing him. The family took me to visit him, and I found him sitting up on his floor mattress, smiling widely. He was extremely frail, and his large smile did not seem to fit his gaunt, wrinkled and gap-toothed face.

I recall us laughing more than talking, but in our relatively short conversation I was able to get a glimpse of what he had been through. His wife for thirty-two years had died just four months before. He had had three children. His first son died at the age of ten when hit by a truck on the highway that ran past the village. His next child, a daughter, married and lived in the same village until she died mysteriously—they thought from a snakebite—two years before, while pregnant with her second child. And his youngest son had rejected his father's Christian faith and had joined a guerrilla movement operating in the southwest part of the country. As if this was not enough, he was now very ill himself and probably did not have much longer to live.

Yet there he sat, telling me about God's faithfulness, his hope and prayers for his son, and his own love for God. And he did all this with exuberance and joy. While I had been taken there to be an encouragement to him in some way, it was instead he who encouraged me. I was the recipient, because he had so much of God to give. In fact, he actually insisted on praying for me on my departure.

Psalms—A Book of Struggle and Celebration

In the midst of all their sufferings, insecurities and worries, Latin American Christians are a people of faith who find endless life in the

Lord of life. They relate especially well to the Old Testament, which deals with the contrasting themes of celebration and oppression. More specifically, they love the Psalms, which express the full range of deep suffering and joy with which they are well acquainted. Furthermore, the Psalms also emphasize a practical side of celebration—that of music and dancing. They reveal that, following times of suffering, life becomes all the more treasured. And life in its richest form for the people of Israel was experienced in the music of praise before the Lord led by singers, instrumentalists and dancers. It was in this way that those given the breath of life drank the cup of life to the full.

Throughout the 150 pieces of Hebrew poetry that make up the Psalms, we see praise and life prevail over struggle and suffering. The Israelites worshiped God with passion. They wept for the rains and danced over the promise of them. They danced and sang over God's gifts of freedom and healing. They held huge festivals with people traveling from all over the country to take part for days on end in ceremonies filled with music, drama and dance.

Dancing and leaping before God was a natural way for the people of the Old Testament to worship God and thank him for life. They saw God as dancing with his creation, indicating their belief that he shared in the joy of his creatures and was committed to the triumph of a joyful life. Even in late antiquity, the Phoenicians had a god known as the "Lord of the Dance."

The Psalms present the celebration of dance as a response to God's faithfulness in providing life. The greatest festival of the Israelites was the autumn festival between September and October, on the brink of the rainy season, when a new cycle of growth was just around the corner. The whole society threw itself into prayer and praise. In ceremonies they reenacted the theme of creation, showing God, the Lord of life, creating the earth and seas. "The Lord is King," went up the cry, and with trumpets, clapping, dancing and prostration the Israelites expressed their faith that he was the Lord of life.

It was a tremendous occasion. The hillsides around the fortress city of Jerusalem, covered with camps of the Israelites, resounded with psalms and acclamations. And the sacred way up to the temple was the scene of many exciting processions. The temple itself, with its bronze pillars and golden-brown stone, shone in the bright sun. Above all, the Israelites worshiped with their hearts. In the Psalms we see life lived to the highest height, the glory of God, the ultimate hallelujah.

Once during a particularly lively worship service in Cuba in which many were dancing, the woman next to me, pausing to catch her breath, said, "You know, my Jesus always dances."

Hispanic Christians have the beautiful gift of seeing everything as coming from God. This enables them to accept the situations of life and rejoice within them.

The God Who Acts *Now*

Hispanic Christians are a faith-filled people who expect to see God's involvement in their lives on a daily basis in practical ways. They have a worldview that easily accepts the supernatural. Their encounter with God is intense. Through his Holy Spirit God invades their lives and takes up residence there, filling life with new meaning. They experience this as a change of life—not in the daily conditions but in their expectations. They begin to see reality through the lens of God's power and expect to see signs of that power at work.

Once on a trip to several countries in Central America I had the opportunity of spending a considerable amount of time in the rural areas away from the large cities. I traveled for a week from village to village with a team showing the *Jesus* film, an evangelistic portrayal of Jesus' life that has been greatly used to touch people's lives all over the world. As I lived among those on the film team and watched different showings, I observed the hand of God at work in the lives not only of the villagers but also of the team members. People became believers, there were physical healings, marriages were mended—time after time they saw answers to the very prayers they had prayed that same week. God was a very real presence in their lives.

I have discovered that many Hispanic Christians love the Emmaus Road story (Lk 24:13-35) because they can relate to Christ who walks with them, listens to their story and shares himself with them. In whatever state they find themselves, they know the Lord is present and expect him to be at work. This makes their faith vibrant, relevant and fresh.

I have been told of a Latin-American Christian leader who insists on having an empty chair in the room when someone meets with him as a living reminder of Jesus' very real presence and to indicate his desire to be sensitive to the leading of the Holy Spirit. It is almost as if, in Latin America, the Christians have spiritual antennae, an extra sensitivity to God's presence and involvement.

As Christians we are those who have discovered "the fountain of life." Latin-American Christians are inspiring, living examples of how to celebrate God's gift of life. And this ability to live in the present results in that extra sensitivity to God's Spirit that all Christians so deeply desire, whether consciously or unconsciously.

In the words of Malcolm Muggeridge:

> We can become new men and women in a new world. . . . It happens, as it has happened innumerable times; it goes on happening. The testimony to this effect is overwhelming. Suddenly caught up in the wonder of God's love, flooding the universe, made aware of the stupendous creativity that animates all life of our own participation in it; every color brighter, every meaning clearer, every shape more shapely, every note more musical, every word written and spoken more explicit. Above all, every human face, all human companionship, all human encounters, recognizably a family affair. The animals too, flying, prowling, burrowing, all their diverse cries and grunts and bellowings, and the majestic hilltops, the gaunt rocks giving their

blessed shade, and the rivers faithfully making their ways to the sea; all irradiated with this same new glory.

What other fulfillment is there that could possibly compare with this? What going to the moon or exploration of the universe? What victory or defeat? What revolution or counter-revolution? What putting down of the mighty from their seat or exalting of the humble and meek? A fulfillment that transcends all human fulfilling, and yet is accessible to all humans. And thus fortified we can laugh . . . nor need we despair.[2]

—4—

Rediscovering Jesus Our Teacher

Christians from the Indian Subcontinent

Have you ever wondered if you are experiencing all that the Christian life has to offer? Many of us have benefited from learning theology, doctrine and church history that Jesus' disciples never had a chance to learn. The disciples did not have the inspired teachings of the apostle Paul in the epistles to the Romans, Corinthians, Galatians, Ephesians and others. Nor did they have the unfolding of the future that we have from John's vision in Revelation. Yet they had something very vital and dynamic. We know the New Testament in a way they did not—for it was not yet written. But they knew the Jesus of the New Testament in a way we have yet to discover and experience. It is this ongoing, ever-deepening discovery of Jesus that makes up the substance of the Christian life and journey.

Christians in South Asia, the Indian subcontinent, perhaps as in no other area of the world, can help Christians in the West to know

Jesus by pointing us toward this road of discovery. Indian Christians keep Jesus as their continual primary focus and see him from a different perspective—a perspective that can provide Western Christians with spiritual freshness. Their Christian faith and orientation toward Jesus show us the means of rediscovering and experiencing him anew.

The Magnetic Attraction of Jesus

Each time I have visited South Asia I have come away revitalized in my understanding and view of Jesus. One of the most interesting conversations I have ever had took place on a train heading toward Bangalore in South India. In my compartment was an Indian physicist who was a high-caste Hindu. While being entirely uninterested in Christianity and the church, he was drawn to the life and teachings of Jesus and confidently referred to him as "the greatest teacher who ever lived." For three whole hours he discoursed on the message and example of "the Great Teacher." When he discovered my personal interest in Jesus, he could not be contained from sharing his own impressions with both passion and sincerity. I came away from my conversation with him reminded afresh that Jesus naturally attracts people to himself. People are fascinated by Jesus.

During a visit to Bangladesh I met a Muslim man who had learned about Jesus from a Christian colleague. He was so drawn to the personality of Jesus that his almost obsessive hunger to learn more had led him to steal a New Testament from a Hindu neighbor. Remarkably, a bestselling book in Muslim Bangladesh has been an "Islamized" or contextually presented New Testament called *Injil Sharif,* the "Holy Gospel" in Qur'anic terminology, demonstrating people's hunger to learn about Jesus. In this Muslim-dominated country an astonishing movement is currently taking place in which hundreds, if not thousands, of individuals have decided on the basis of their Qur'anic and Injilic readings to follow Jesus rather than

Muhammad. These people have not adopted any of the traditions of Western Christian worship and therefore do not call themselves Christians; they simply refer to themselves as "followers of Jesus."

Whether visiting and working in Muslim Bangladesh, Hindu India or Buddhist Sri Lanka, I have always come away from South Asia with a fresh reminder that Jesus naturally attracts people to himself. Many are not interested in the Christian traditions in which Jesus is often presented, or the Western Jesus that we have created over the centuries—he bores some to death. However, many are interested in the raw Jesus, the Jesus as he is presented in the Gospels. The words of the apostle Paul take on new meaning in this context: "For I resolved to know nothing while I was with you except Jesus Christ and him crucified" (1 Cor 2:2). "For we do not preach ourselves, but Jesus Christ as Lord" (2 Cor 4:5). This has resulted in changing my understanding and manner of sharing the Christian faith—encouraging a study of the life of Christ rather than Christian theology or doctrine.

In 1925 a fascinating book was written by E. Stanley Jones, a distinguished missionary and evangelist to India, entitled *The Christ of the Indian Road.* It raises the questions, "How was and is Jesus understood and in what way does he go down India's roads?" The central theme is that Christianity and Jesus are not necessarily the same thing. One can have Jesus without the system that has been built up around him in the West—and vice versa.

The gospel, the good news, lies in the person of Jesus. He himself is this good news, and a Christian is one who follows him, lives for him and presents him as the good news. After all, the term "Christianity" is not found in the Scriptures, and Jesus was not a Christian. The term "Christian" did not come to be used until new followers of Jesus began gathering in Antioch in Syria, years after his death.

The essence of Christianity is Christ. Our starting point as Christians is Christ. Start at any other place and we inevitably get off track. And Christ is also our finishing point. Our entire objective is to be like Christ. Christ is the center of Christianity—a full commitment to him, catching his mind and spirit, and living his life, constitutes being a Christian. There is a tremendous difference between Christian revelation, which is Christ, and Christian religion, which is Christianity. A problem of the church in the West is that, instead of presenting the truth of Christ, she has often tried to present Christianity as a better faith or religion—which is not necessarily the case. If anything about Christianity is true, it is true because of Christ—not because of Christianity.

While Christians—especially Protestants—are often called a "people of the book," a more accurate title should be "people of a Person." We value the Bible as an inspired record of God's revelation, but the revelation itself is the person of Jesus Christ. Christianity has nothing to do with knowing a creed or doctrine or living a certain lifestyle. Rather, it has everything to do with knowing a person.

Time spent in the Indian subcontinent has served to remind me that many in the West do not have anything against Christ but rather against both the religious trappings of Christianity and the actions of Christians. When these negative views and experiences are revealed as unrelated to the true person of Christ, people become interested in Jesus.

As Christians we are loyal to someone we have found to be the truth. This conviction runs so deep that we would agree with the Russian writer Dostoevsky when he wrote to a friend in 1854 saying, "If anyone proved to me that Christ was outside the truth, and it really was so that the truth was outside Christ, then I would prefer to remain with Christ than with the truth." As Christians, at the heart of our faith must be the deepest and yet simplest conviction about this person named Jesus.

Those of us living in the West can easily have a view of Jesus that is so set in fixed and stereotyped ways that we are only able to see certain sides of him. South Asian Christians help us pull off our blinders, enabling us to see Jesus in a newer and truer light. Bishop John Robinson, in his 1979 book *Truth Is Two-Eyed,* said: "It is in fact in Christology [the study of Christ] that, I suspect, most is to be learnt from Indian Christian writers." Christians on the Indian subcontinent have much to teach and show us about Jesus Christ.

It was not long after the founding of the church in the Middle East that Christian congregations appeared in India. For two millennia, tucked away in the midst of a vast Hindu population, the Nestorian Church of St. Thomas has existed in India. This church finds its origins in the first century when Thomas (the doubting disciple) came as a missionary to southern India. Tradition says Thomas was martyred in what is today the city of Meliapore in India.

This ancient church—as well as the many other churches that have worked in India throughout the centuries—will tell you that it was and is a cultural and religious necessity to focus on the person of Jesus in sharing the Christian faith. Hindus are not impressed by personal experience or testimony—they view religious experience as normal. Neither are Hindus taken aback by the miraculous, as they are familiar with the many accounts of supernatural wonders in their own religious literature. Nothing has spoken as powerfully and generated as much interest as Christ's personality and teachings. As a result Indian Christians over the years have found that the best advice a Christian can give to someone searching spiritually is simply to encourage them to follow the historical Jesus, trusting that in so doing they will encounter the divinity of Jesus.

Mahatma Gandhi called his autobiography *The Story of My Experiments with Truth.* Throughout it you discover his fascination with Jesus. He was given the Bible at a young age and started reading it from the beginning. He said: "I read the book of Genesis, and the chapters that followed invariably sent me to sleep. . . . I disliked reading the book of Numbers. But the New Testament produced a different impression, especially the Sermon on the Mount, which went straight to my heart."[1] There was a deep strain of Christian thought and practice running through Gandhi's life. He was drawn to the person of Christ and Christ's teachings. The words of Jesus delighted him. Hindu fundamentalists even accused him of being a secret Christian, which he considered a compliment.

He regarded Jesus as the highest *Satyagrahi,* one absolutely devoted to following the truth. Satyagraha, meaning "truth force," was the idea and practice at the center of Gandhi's life. This "truth force" was in essence the way of the cross. One of his favorite songs was "When I Survey the Wondrous Cross." This led to Gandhi, a non-Christian, becoming one of the most Christlike men in history. He embraced Christ and his teachings, regarding Jesus as one of the greatest teachers of mankind, but rejected Christianity, remaining a "semi-Hindu."

Among the many who came literally to sit at Gandhi's feet were Christian missionaries—and his evident respect for and interest in Christ made many Christians in India reanalyze their own faith and commitment. In this sense Gandhi, a non-Christian, through his life, helped to "Christianize unchristian Christianity."[2]

Sadhu Sundar Singh, an influential Indian Christian mystic who died in 1928, was a man consumed by the person and presence of Christ. He was once interviewed by an agnostic European professor of comparative religions in a Hindu college. The evident intention of the interview was to show the Sadhu (holy man) his mistake in leaving another faith for Christ. "What have you found in Christianity that you did not have in your old religion?" the professor asked. The Sadhu said, "I have Christ." "Yes, I know," the professor replied, a little impatiently. "But what particular principle or doctrine have you found that you did not have before?" The Sadhu answered, "The particular thing I have found is Christ."[3]

Sadhu Sundar Singh writes:

> When people ask me, "What made you a Christian?" I can only say:
> "Christ Himself made me a Christian." When he revealed himself to
> me I saw his glory and was convinced that he was the Living Christ. I
> do not believe in Jesus Christ because I have read about him in the
> Bible—I saw him and experienced him and know him in my daily
> experience. Not because I read the Gospels, but because of him of
> whom I read in the Gospels, have I become what I am. Already
> before my conversion I loved his teaching; it is beautiful. But my
> doubts were not swept away until I became aware that Christ was.[4]

For the Sadhu, his entire faith was a communion with the person of
Christ.

On one of my trips to India I visited a church of converted Hindus
in the slums of Calcutta. It was located in the Kumartuli area, where
thousands of Hindu idols are made. We sang together and shared
with each other our stories of God's faithfulness. In poverty and
unemployment these young men and women had nothing but their
faith in Christ. It was all they could call their own. In situations like
this I come to realize that the only thing we really do have in common to talk about, once all the irrelevant Western cultural traditions,
terminology and trappings of our faith are removed, is Christ. In this
small "church" that met in a one-room house, as we were singing a
Bengali chorus, I was profoundly struck by the realization that these
people were here only because of Christ. There was no other incen-
tive to attend. Christ had drawn them to himself. The young Bengali
lay pastor, Swapan Dasgupta, echoed my sentiments when he said
after the service:

> I have daily visited homes, braving rain and storm and slushy roads. I
> have learned a great deal from the people of Calcutta—that in this
> busy city, people are not only interested in making a living or involv-
> ing themselves in politics, but are eager to know about Jesus Christ
> who alone can truly change lives.

Consequently, he was seeing small groups of new Christians meeting to worship together in some very unlikely places, including even an idol workshop.

Also in Calcutta is the society—the Missionaries of Charity—begun by Mother Teresa, an Albanian born in Serbia. She lived and worked among the extremely poor in India for most of her life. "I feel Indian to the most profound depths of my soul," she once said.[5] When meeting her I could not help but realize that her whole orientation in life centers around the person of Christ:

> Jesus explains our Life. When a visitor comes to our house, I take him to the chapel to pray a while. I tell him, "Let us first greet the master of the house. Jesus is here." Keep giving Jesus to your people . . . by your being in love with Jesus.[6]

Indian Christians remind us again and again that it is not our Scriptures, church or doctrine that make Christianity unique among the world's religions—but it is Christ. Consequently our mission as Christians is entirely focused around him—following him, sharing him, becoming like him. It is Christ who should be highlighted above all else in our lives.

Wilhelm Bousset, a scholar of the history of religions in the early 1900s who strongly influenced the great German theologian Rudolf Bultmann, said, "Whenever Christianity has struck out a new path in her journey it has been because the personality of Jesus has again become living, and a ray of his being has once more illumined the world." This echoes Jesus' statement about himself, "When I am lifted up from the earth, [I] will draw all people to myself" (Jn 12:32).

In focusing primarily on Jesus Christ, South Asian Christians view him very differently than we do in the West. They picture Jesus with brown skin and in deep thought; very contemplative in his manner, even at times portrayed as sitting in a cross-legged lotus position. After all, Jesus came from western Asia. They make a point of this, in contrast to the European image of Jesus often presented by missionaries—a young man with pale skin, blue eyes and light-brown beard and hair.

Gandhi thought that Christianity became disfigured when it went westward during its first several hundred years, becoming "the religion of kings."[7] Hence Aloysius Pieris, a Sri Lankan theologian, speaks of "our desperate search for the Asian face of Christ."[8]

Jesus—A Living Teacher

This Asian face of Christ, for Indian Christians, takes the form of Jesus as a teacher who was not only the greatest of teachers (at one specific time) but who also lives and teaches them in the present. This fits perfectly into their culture, which is very teacher-orientated. India is renowned for its *gurus, sadhus* (holy men), *roshis* (prophets) and *swamis* (teaching lords) with their *chelas* (disciples).

For years now it has been fashionable for Westerners to go to the East, to India, in search of spiritual wisdom and guidance. The temples and ashrams in South Asia have been receiving men and women from the West by the thousands. And from South Asia any number of gurus and roshis are traveling to the West, to Europe and the United States, to give instruction and guidance according to the religious traditions of Asia.

While traveling through India on one trip I twice crossed paths with two German women. They had specifically come to India looking for a guru to tutor them. The first time I saw them was in Bangalore, and they had just spent several days sitting at the feet of Sai Baba, a guru-type living not far from Bangalore who caters to Western seekers. They were obviously unimpressed with his teachings. They were soon to leave for Calcutta to visit some other guru whose name was not familiar to me. I suggested that while they were there they also sit at the feet of Mother Teresa. About two weeks later I saw them for a second time in Madras. In recounting their adventures they told me that they had spent four days with Mother Teresa's Missionaries of Charity. They were awed by the sense of spiritual depth in the community and, before knowing I was a Christian, informed me, "You must first follow Jesus in order to follow Mother Teresa."

India is known for its ashrams, places of religious retreat and instruction where a guru lives with and teaches his disciples or chelas. These ashrams attracted so much interest among Indians that Christian ashrams began to be founded in 1917. This development of Indian Christian communities fitted perfectly into the local Indian religious culture. The ashram might have a Christian sadhu as its leader, but residents and visitors alike were pointed toward following "Swami Jesus," (swami meaning "Lord who teaches"). Many Indian Christians refer to Jesus as their Swami.

At the beginning of Mark's Gospel we see Jesus defining himself as a teacher (Mk 1:21-28). He is beginning his ministry and chooses to do so in a synagogue, the primary Judaic teaching institution. A Jewish synagogue service consisted of three components: prayer, the reading of Scripture and the exposition of it. There was no music, singing or sacrifice. Worship and sacrifices were offered only at the temple, while the synagogues served as places of teaching and instruction. Since there was only one temple and it was in Jerusalem, the synagogues were in fact more influential. Wherever there was a colony of ten Jewish families, a synagogue was built. If a teacher had a message to share, the synagogue served as his platform.

While each synagogue had certain religious officials, there was no permanent teacher. At a service it was up to the ruler—the man responsible for the general administration—to call on any competent person to give the address and scriptural exposition. In this sense there was no professional teaching ministry. Jesus, therefore, found it quite easy to open his kingdom campaign in a synagogue.

He became an itinerant rabbi, teaching publicly in the synagogues of Galilee, privately in the homes of friends or in the natural arenas provided by the rolling hillsides; he even used a fishing boat as his platform. Nicodemus, a Pharisee who visited him in secret, called him "Rabbi" and "teacher . . . from God" (Jn 3:2). Even Judas as he approached Jesus in the Garden of Gethsemane to betray him said "Greetings, Rabbi" (Mt 26:49).

He spoke with unparalleled eloquence and authority. His invitation to discipleship proved irresistible to eleven Galileans and one Judean, as well as to a wider circle of some seventy followers. Women were also prominent among his followers and even supported him financially. Most who heard him speak were deeply impressed by his teachings. He dined with the rich and drank with the poor. His words attracted fishermen and tax collectors, high officials in government and lepers, those with open minds and those too burdened to understand. His teaching ministry took him from the shores of the Sea of Galilee to the Mediterranean coast and the borders of Lebanon.

Jesus accurately reflected the contemporary cultural understanding of a teacher. The culture at that time was one of teachers and rabbis who had disciples with them in a well-defined and special relationship. Several aspects of the rabbi-disciple relationship in first-century Judaism are very significant in understanding Jesus' teaching role—and they help us to see how Indian Christians find the person of Jesus so enthralling.

A disciple in first-century Palestine would typically have left home and moved in with the teacher. This provides some background to the statement in Luke's Gospel that Jesus' disciples left everything and followed him (Lk 14:26). Furthermore, the disciple would serve a teacher in the most servantlike manner, acknowledging the teacher's absolute authority. Within this setup the disciple was expected not only to learn all that the rabbi knew but also to become like him in character and lifestyle. Jesus maintained an intimate tutorial setup with his disciples. The disciples observed his life while traveling with him. He answered their questions about a day's events and questioned them in turn.

Indian Christians view themselves as disciples of Swami Jesus, often avoiding the label "Christian" because of its connotations in their local context (it brings to mind the former relationship between Western colonialism and missionary expansion). They would rather call themselves fully devoted "followers of Jesus." Some of them use the Hindu word *gurukulam* to describe their orientation to following Jesus. *Gurukulam* is the principle of active learning through a personal relationship between a teacher and a pupil. Many Christians in South Asia have come to the Christian faith through studying the life and teachings of Jesus the teacher. Then after they come to faith, he becomes their personal and present divine teacher or swami, a living teacher-Lord.

So often in the West we view Jesus as having been a teacher once upon a time, in the past tense, and we look today to be taught primarily from his teachings back then—teachings found in the Gospels and also reflected in the Epistles, contemporary Christian literature, the words of Christian leaders and the lessons of church history. Indian Christians, however, view Jesus as their active teacher in the present moment—their current primary source of spiritual growth. To them his most significant teachings are not back then but are being received in the present tense, the today, even if still through the Scriptures.

Sadhu Sundar Singh beautifully illustrated this through his life and message. He constantly referred to himself as "sitting at the Master's feet." He once said:

> Sit at the Master's feet in prayer; it is the greatest theological college in this world. We know about theology, but He is the source of theology itself. He explains in a few seconds a truth that has taken years to

understand. Whatever I have learnt has been only at His feet.[9]

Indian Christians are right in their view of Jesus: he is and should all the more be our teacher today. This is not generally the Western approach, and yet it is fundamental to our spiritual development. E. Stanley Jones explained the need for this tutorial perspective when he said, "Christ and the [individual] are made for one another, and when they are brought together, deep speaks to deep and wounds answer wounds."[10]

As Christians we are students in his eternal classroom. Before coming to faith we could say we were at the undergraduate level. On becoming a believer, a fully devoted follower of Jesus, we begin our postgraduate studies. And the studying and schooling go on and on; we never finish. We are always on new and different courses, each with varying degrees of difficulty, while always having the same professor and tutor. The subject of study is the same: Christlikeness. Jesus defined his goal of discipleship when he said, "A student is not above his teacher, but everyone who is fully trained will be like his teacher" (Lk 6:40). Likeness—not just knowledge—was the goal of Jewish discipleship. Therefore likeness to Jesus is the goal God the Father has for us.

Jesus continues to teach us and show us how we should live, through the Holy Spirit who was sent to clarify and personalize to us Jesus' teachings (Jn 14:26). This is what the apostle Paul meant when he said "We . . . are being transformed into [Jesus'] likeness with ever-increasing glory" (2 Cor 3:18).

Jesus—An Unorthodox Teacher

Not only do Indian Christians view Jesus as their supreme living teacher, but they also recognize him as a teacher with unorthodox and unconventional teaching methods.

Those who saw the film *Dead Poets Society,* starring Robin Williams, can never forget his role as an unconventional teacher. I recall one scene when he was teaching English literature, and he read aloud the introduction of their textbook with which he disagreed. He then ordered his students to rip the introduction out of the book— and they all did so in unison, though hesitantly. On another occasion he asked his students in the classroom, "Language was developed for one endeavor, and that is?" One student quickly answered, "To communicate," to which Robin Williams responded, "To woo women!" It was through the unconventionality of his teaching that the students began to learn, understand and love the subject as never before.

The Gospel writer Mark begins his account of the life of Christ by showing that Jesus was entirely unconventional in the way he communicated himself. This is illustrated right from the outset by Mark's depiction of the way in which Jesus dealt with evil spirits (Mk 1:23-26). The ordinary Jewish or pagan exorcist used elaborate incantations, spells and magical formulas. The Middle East at that time was full of people who could exorcise demons, more often than not in very strange ways. For example, they would put a ring under the oppressed person's nose, recite a long spell, and then splash in a basin of water, or use a "magical" root called *baaras*.

Jesus, however, exorcised the demon from the man with one word of clear, simple, brief authority. The onlookers were astonished at Jesus' power. They had not seen anything like it before. The power was not in the spell, formula or incantation. It was in Jesus.

Jesus was most unconventional in his teaching methods, which were varied and complex. He conversed, asked and answered questions, taught in obscure parables, and spoke on mountains or from boats. He also made shocking statements to get his listeners to think seriously about an issue. One such incident was his statement that"the Sabbath was made for man, not man for the Sabbath" (Mk 2:27). This was extremely provocative, completely contrary to the religious culture of the day. And extraordinary phenomena often accompanied his teaching.

His miracles fell into different categories. More than half related to physical healings—healings from diseases and disabilities. Others were psychological and spiritual in orientation, such as exorcisms. Still others were life-restoring, when he resurrected the dead, giving new life. He performed miracles relating to nature as well as people, quieting terrible storms, walking on water and turning water into wine. He used each miracle as an aid or illustration in his teaching.

Indians are quite used to the extraordinary in their gurus' teachings. I remember visiting Sai Baba, a guru who teaches outside Bangalore in South India. Sai Baba, a gifted illusionist, spent a considerable amount of time doing magic or sleight-of-hand tricks to awe those in attendance.

Christians in South Asia, therefore, have little problem with Christ's extraordinary and unorthodox ways of communicating and teaching. They have a beautiful way of describing these occurrences, calling them "heavenly surprises." Western critical rationalism, which is skeptical about the supernatural, can hamper our understanding of these things, whereas Indian Christians can accept them all without any difficulty.

Sadhu Sundar Singh moved in the world of miracles. He felt that stories of the supernatural in his own life existed to strengthen and develop his own Christian faith and that of others. Once he was sitting lost in the middle of a jungle on the bank of a rushing river, not knowing what to do. An unknown man appeared and swam across with him on his back—and then disappeared. At another time he was sleeping outside at night, shivering and very hungry, when two strangers brought him food; as he went to thank them, they vanished. Once men armed with sticks surrounded him and began to beat him. He prayed—and when he opened his eyes they had gone. These men returned the next morning and asked him about the "men in shining garments" who had aided him. Once, in Tibet, Buddhists bound him to a tree in the forest and left him throughout a very cold night. When he awoke in the morning he found a pile of fruit at his side and his chains lying on the ground. Another time he was put in a well full of dead bodies for three days. An unknown man pulled him out, healed his injured arm and then vanished. The key to the well's cover was found to be still hanging on the persecuting judges' clothes.[11]

Whenever he described his many miraculous experiences, he always stressed the importance of the deeper lessons learned through them. When speaking about his release from his chains in the forest, he said:

> The most wonderful part of the whole experience was not the fact that I was set free, but that I was allowed to feel this wonderful peace in the midst of those terrible sufferings. . . . I have often met people who wanted me to talk about this sort of thing, and they wanted me to tell them some stories. But the greatest miracle of all is the fact that Jesus Christ has changed my whole nature.[12]

God used miraculous, unorthodox and extraordinary occurrences to help his servant grow toward Christlikeness.

In the slum churches of Calcutta I met a Christian man who worked in a large Hindu idol factory. It was the only job available to him, yet he shared how he felt wrong about making idols in which he no longer believed. He decided to leave his work on the day when something extraordinary happened: while he was putting the eyes on the Hindu idol, as he had done countless times before, he saw Jesus looking at him through the idol's eyes. At that moment, he said, he knew that his work was an abomination to God.

Jesus, our divine teacher, uses both the ordinary and extraordinary to develop our faith. He loves to surprise us, astonish us, catch us off guard, even shock us, and in so doing always shares more of his character and nature, as well as showing us how we can follow him more closely.

Jesus—A Teacher Whose Subject Is Himself

Most teachers or gurus teach a subject in which others in the world have some significant knowledge and expertise as well. The difference with Jesus is that he is the only one who can teach us about himself.

Mark, in the first part of his Gospel, shows us how much Jesus' teaching differed from that of the scribes (Mk 1:27-28). Jesus taught with *personal* authority. No scribe ever gave a decision on his own. Rather, he would always begin, "There is a teaching that . . . ," and then he would quote all the relevant authorities. The last thing a scribe ever gave was an individually determined judgment. The prophets always began with "The LORD says," and rabbis had to cite a Scripture passage for everything they said.

Jesus operated very differently. When he spoke, it was as if he needed no authority beyond himself. He spoke with complete independence, citing no authorities and quoting no experts. Christ spoke with the finality of the voice of God.

At that time, a disciple in Judaism had to master not only the Scriptures but also the oral and written traditions that had grown up around the Scriptures. Only after being taught in this way could a person become a rabbi or teach with any authority. This is why the Jews were amazed at Jesus' teaching. Jesus taught with authority— without having gone through the only process that the Jews felt could qualify anyone to teach. This is the significance of the people's saying of Jesus, "How did this man get such learning without having studied?" (Jn 7:15).

It was his sheer authority that staggered people. He was authority incarnate. He was his message. This is why, when an evil spirit said, "You are—the Holy One of God," Jesus told him, "Be quiet!" (Lk 4:34-35), as he wanted to reveal this to the people himself. He himself as the revelation of the nature of God was the subject of his teaching. Luke records Jesus explaining to his disciples "what was said in all the Scriptures concerning himself" (Lk 24:27). This comes out most strongly during the week before his crucifixion. It is significant that three of the four Gospels devote a full third of their content to reporting on this last week. And the fourth (John) dedicates its entire second half to this period, emphasizing that Jesus' teaching focused on himself as the Son of God. That note of personal authority rang out, and it is a note that captures the ears of people.

While in Colombo, Sri Lanka, I met two former Buddhist monks. As monks they used to have their heads shaved and wear orange robes. While at their monastery they were given a New Testament, which they began to study. They found themselves strongly drawn to the person of Jesus and the inherent authority evident in his teachings. Through time they became convinced that his authority was due to his divinity, the fact that he was the Son of God. They then studied further in the New Testament to learn how believers in Jesus should follow him and began to focus on the Acts of the Apostles. In so doing, they came to the conclusion that they needed to be baptized, and they approached a Christian minister in Colombo who ended up baptizing them. These two men now visit Buddhist monks, helping them study and learn from this living teacher, Jesus Christ.

When Christ speaks and teaches, people know it is beyond human argument, for it is the voice of God. And he keeps on speaking and teaching. There is never a point in our spiritual life and theology when we do not have to keep learning from him. For we can never fully comprehend all the knowledge of God, nor ever reach a totally Christlike life. Jesus must be allowed to be our living teacher if we are to grow in spiritual depth.

I will never forget the photographs I saw in Bangladesh after one of the recurring cyclones had brought devastation. One picture showed a Hindu man whose home had been destroyed by the flooding. He had lost all he owned and was standing in what was once his one-room house, holding on to the remaining center pole with one hand. In his other hand he was clutching a New Testament. It was clear that he felt there was a certain power in Jesus Christ that he needed at that time of crisis.

The well-known German theologian and missionary Albert Schweitzer wrote at the end of his book *The Quest of the Historical Jesus:*

> He comes to us as One unknown, without a name, as of old, by the lakeside, He came to those men who knew him not. He speaks to us the same words: "Follow me. . . ." To those who obey him, wise or simple, he will reveal himself in the labours, conflicts, and miseries they will experience. . . . As an ineffable mystery, they shall come inwardly to know who he is.

Mother Teresa of Calcutta said, "To me Jesus is my God, Jesus is my Power, Jesus is my Life, Jesus is my Love, Jesus is my All in All, Jesus is my Everything."[13] We follow him, not because of anything he said, but because of everything that he is. For as H. G. Wells wrote in his *Outline of History,* summing up the influence of Jesus upon history, "The Galilean has been too great for our small hearts."

A Bengali Hymn
O Christ, the light of the way of my life, abide with me.
When I go into a dense forest I cannot find the way,
O Christ, the guide of the way of my life, show me the way.
My fellow-travelers have deserted me and darkness is all around.
O compassionate Christ, come, or else I will lose my life.
O Christ, the only help of the way of my life, hold my hand.
When the wild storm comes in the river of my life,
my oar is broken and the rudder is torn,
O Christ the boatman! . . . Sit and hold the oar
or else the boat will sink.
O Christ, the oarsman of the boat of my life,
hold the oar.

Written by Nirod Kumar Biswas, a doctor, poet, musician and former bishop of Assam.[14]

—5—

An Invitation
to Freedom

*Africa's Experience
of Liberation*

I *grew up in Africa. It is my heart's home, and naturally, it has* influenced the shaping of my worldview more than any other place. As the great explorer and missionary David Livingstone said in Cambridge in 1857, "I beg to direct your attention to Africa."

"*Ex Africa semper aliquid novi,*" exclaimed Julius Caesar—"Out of Africa always something new." Today Africa is the fastest-growing Christian continent in the world. While every day in the West, roughly 7,500 people in effect abandon their faith, each day in Africa over double that number become Christians. David Barrett, an Anglican researcher and editor of the *World Christian Encyclopedia*, estimates that each year more than six million Africans are added to the church, with about two-fifths being new converts. It has been estimated that Africa will have nearly 325 million Christians in the year 2000. This makes the Christian church probably the most powerful institution in sub-Saharan Africa today.

The African prophet Blyden said over a century ago that Africa was "the spiritual reservoir of the world." We have much to learn from African Christians who have a tremendous faith. And I agree wholeheartedly with the late American Bishop Fulton Sheen when he said, "God's next tune will be played on the black keys." Within God's African tune is a refrain about the people's experience of God's freedom.

Freedom has frequently been headline news over the last decade. Since the breaching of the Berlin Wall in 1989 freedom seems to have broken out everywhere, often in very unlikely places—throughout Eastern Europe and the former Soviet Union, in Namibia, Mozambique and even in South Africa where Nelson Mandela not only walked free but has gone on to lead his country to political freedom.

There is another type of freedom, however, that everyone is also searching and longing for—an inner, personal freedom. Jesus promised, "If the Son sets you free, you will be free indeed" (Jn 8:36). The longer I am a Christian, and the more I get to know both Christ and myself, the more I realize that in Christianity freedom relates to every part of me, the complete me—spiritually, emotionally, psychologically, physically.

How often do we dream of what it would be like to be really free? We long to escape the darkness that is part of all our lives. As Christians we can thank God that every once in a while we have had our own dreams of freedom—of the individual we might be, who we dream of being. Just suppose we were able to forever rid ourselves of each thing that holds us back, that weighs us down—the things we have done and continue to do or fail to do, that hurt us or appear to kill a part of us. Suppose we could untie them all and let them fall off! To dream like that is very difficult because in one sense it seems so possible, only just out of our reach—and yet in another sense it seems further than the most distant, remote country.

We often feel so trapped in a particular area of our lives that we can see no way out. The psalmist described this feeling when he said, "I am confined and cannot escape; my eyes are dim with grief" (Ps 88:8–9). It can seem like hell at times—a place or life situation from which we cannot escape, a place of misery and anguish. We can well identify with the Michelangelo slave sculpture in the Galleria dell' Accademia in Florence: the figure is only partially carved out of the stone because the artist wanted to express its trapped condition. Michelangelo had a beautiful explanation as to why sculpting from marble-block was his favorite genre: he said he felt as if he was "freeing a figure that was imprisoned in the stone."

It was in Burkina-Faso, West Africa, where I was stranded due to a coup d'état, that I first read Robert Louis Stevenson's well-known story *The Strange Case of Dr. Jekyll and Mr. Hyde.* This tale brilliantly succeeds in capturing the tension between our two natures. Dr. Henry Jekyll, a genteel London physician, concocts a drug that changes his personality to conform completely to his evil side, thereby becoming Mr. Hyde, the physical representation of his evil self. In this way he begins to live a double life. The story gradually reveals the powerful tensions between his two natures, his good and evil sides. Dr. Jekyll struggles to resist Mr. Hyde, his evil representation, but eventually his evil nature gains the upper hand and Mr. Hyde kills himself.

This sense of captivity within us is what the apostle Paul describes in Romans 7, where he writes about our experience of a lack of freedom. He says, "For what I do is not the good thing I want to do; no, the evil I do not want to do—this I keep on doing" (Rom 7:19).

Yet Paul also talks about the vital importance of discovering true freedom. This theme runs throughout the Bible but can be most clearly seen in Romans 8. Paul describes the desire of creation and of human beings in particular to free themselves from all that prevents them from being like God. He describes creation as groaning, in frustration, to free itself from every chain to take part in the "glorious freedom of the children of God" (Rom 8:21). To write with such certainty Paul must have tasted of God's freedom.

The salvation that Christ brings is a total liberation allowing us to belong fully in God's kingdom. And the Christian journey is a road to experiencing greater and greater freedom. Every once in a while we are blessed with a fresh sense of deliverance, a more profound release, which encourages us to journey on, seeking more.

Freedom is perhaps what we hunger for more than anything else, but it is often the last thing we seem able to obtain. We live in a world of hurting people. Many feel as restricted as if their hands and feet were chained together. Others feel they have to hide behind masks, concealing their real situations. The good news is that God is in the business of setting people free and giving them new beginnings. He loves us too much to leave us the way we are. And the question always before us is, "Are we experiencing more of God's freedom in our Christian life?"

Christianity in Africa proposes and proclaims a message of God's liberation. African Christians have a greater experiential understanding of God's freedom than any other Christians I have met anywhere in the world. The freedom that Jesus gives them is not so much a doctrine that is preached as an experience that is realized.

Richard Gray, an expert in African history, says, "One of the deepest and most enduring desires of all African societies is the anxiety to eliminate evil."[1] Therefore, Christianity is regarded by believers in Africa as a new and ultimate source of supernatural power, capable of fighting evil successfully and effectively to bring freedom. To them "evil" means anything limiting, besetting or destroying life.

I remember sitting in a discussion about the Christian faith in Senegal, West Africa, when a young Muslim man made a decision to believe in and follow Jesus Christ. Immediately I began thinking about all the difficulties he might face. He would probably be ostracized by his family, losing his social status—and maybe worse. For in his Islamic background it was sometimes considered that "a dead Muslim is better than a living Christian." There had been cases where families tried to end the life of a son or daughter before he or she became too Christianized. This young man was reminded of all these possible ramifications of his decision. Yet he just sat there with such a deep sense of peace and calm, his face almost glowing. I spoke with him afterward about his sense of peace, and he explained that he was simply thinking about all that he had been freed from. He experienced coming to faith as "an indescribable release."

God Is Freedom

African Christians have a strong and clear understanding that the very essence of God's character is freedom. They see God for who he is, that he longs to free us. God is freedom. This is the essence of the gospel—God rescuing, liberating humanity. Christians in Africa accord with the words of the former Anglican archbishop of Cape Town, Desmond Tutu: "Say to yourselves in your heart, 'God loves me . . . I am of infinite value to God.' God created me for freedom . . . freedom is God-given."[2]

Conversion, or coming to the Christian faith, is only the halfway point, however. In a sense it is halftime. The first half finds us losing, while struggling to win. At halftime the coach gives us the winning game plan that we inwardly accept, digest and agree to implement. Then the second half finds us putting into practice the winning strategy, until the ultimate victory is won in eternity.

Once when visiting the United Nations headquarters in Geneva, I saw a most moving sculpture of an African slave carved by an African artist. The slave had been chained to a huge ball, but the chain was broken and lay at his feet; he was free. I found it a powerful reminder of what African Christians have experienced.

The true Christ is one who breaks the binding power of the chains, the one who comes alongside prisoners and frees them. The image of Christ that is most vivid to African Christians is that of Christ the liberator in all dimensions of life, Christ the healer par excellence of their fears, concerns and diseases, Christ as the one who sets his people free in the here and now.

It is very important for us as Christians to study and know the character of God so that we can allow him to play the role he wants in our lives. Of the countless attributes of God there is one facet in particular through which we are able to see his many other facets, and which thereby serves as a strategic viewpoint from where we can see his personality. God is first and foremost, above and beyond anything else, committed to freeing us. This specific presentation of God's character is evident throughout the Old and New Testaments. Yet just as he is our Savior only when we allow him to be our Savior, so also he is our liberator only when we allow him that role in our lives. Western Christians, however, tend to be far more focused these days on trying to free themselves. This is clear from the plethora of "how-to" self-help books in Christian bookstores, telling us how to win freedom in this or that area of our lives. In contrast to the Western presumption that we can save ourselves, the African Christian asks for complete salvation from God. I tried once to find a Christian book on personal suffering written in French but from an African perspective for a seminary student in the Central African Republic. I spent months looking everywhere as I traveled the African continent, but the only books I could find addressed the more general topic of evil in the world. While hundreds, perhaps even thousands, of Christian self-help books exist in the West, I could not find one that originated in Africa. To the African Christian freedom starts with God. So often our Western Christian self-help ideas miss that starting point, meaning that any outcome can only be temporary.

Joseph—A Life of Freedom

The story of Joseph, the flamboyant Old Testament patriarch who spent most of his life in Africa, is an extended exposition of freedom. We are shown how God freed him over and over again, when he could have been enchained by so many things—hatred, resentment, adultery and wealth, among other things. Each time God freed him, we see that he was then able to enter the next phase of life God had planned for him.

Joseph understood God's character and allowed him to play the role of liberator in his life. He was free to dream God's dreams in the midst of the hostility of his entire family. His brothers sold him as a slave to the Arabs, but God freed him by enabling him to become the administrator of Potiphar's estate in Egypt with responsibility over all that Potiphar owned. Later he was freed from the temptation to sleep with Potiphar's beautiful wife—though ironically, this freedom meant being taken from Potiphar's house and thrown into prison.

While in prison he was freed from slave labor by the warden, who put him in charge of the other prisoners. In prison of all places he met Pharaoh's cupbearer, and eventually this friendship freed Joseph to stand in Pharaoh's court. When Pharaoh asked Joseph to interpret his dream, God freed Joseph from his dilemma by giving him the interpretation. Once again he was set free and put in charge not only of the palace but eventually of all Egypt; he became, in effect, the prime minister. Later in his life he was freed from the remembrance of all the past suffering he had undergone—he named his son "Manasseh," meaning "one who forgets." His release from past hurts is also shown in his kind and compassionate treatment of his brothers who had dealt with him cruelly, when he met them again later in life. God continually set him free, and it is clear that Joseph must surely have believed in God as a liberator.

Desmond Tutu says: "To the victims . . . it is important to present

God as the God who has power and not only as a God who will bring freedom. . . . He is not without power though everything seems to prove the contrary. . . . Our God has heard and seen our afflictions and has come to free us."[3] African Christianity puts a very strong emphasis on a triumphant God and a victorious, conquering Christ, who cares, protects and restores us, and who banishes fear. Christ fights against and triumphs over the powers of Satan—disease, hatred, fear and even death itself. He is a healer, miracle worker and protector against evil powers.

When African Christians are asked why they find Christ as conqueror or victor so attractive, their answer is that African Christians are very conscious of the many powers at work in their lives and world: spirits, witchcraft, magic, religious pressure, fear, anxiety, sin, diseases, the forces of evil and the greatest of all—death. East African theologian John Mbiti says, "Africans see that invisible universe when they look at, hear or feel the visible and tangible world."[4]

To Africans the power of Jesus encounters the hollow power of demons, spirits, witches or sorcerers, and the powers of sickness, poverty and death—the powers of evil in all its individual and structural manifestations. The words to a popular Christian song from the Transvaal area of Southern Africa loudly echo this perspective on Jesus:

Jesus Christ is conqueror,
by his resurrection he overcame death itself,
by his resurrection he overcame all things:
he overcame magic,
he overcame amulets and charms,
he overcame the darkness of demon-possession,
he overcame dread.
When we are with him,
We also conquer.

Some of an African's worst fears can be those of breaking cultural or tribal taboos, fearing the consequences to themselves and their families. They often interpret the events in their lives in terms of magic and the power of evil spirits and therefore feel imprisoned, held by many fears. Many African Christians have been freed from those fears by the power of the gospel. They find a fresh intimacy with Christ, who frees them and gives them an unprecedented sense of happiness and release. A popular Nigerian chorus goes "Jesus' Power—Super Power. Satan's Power—Powerless Power."

The history of African Christianity reflects this approach to the Christian faith. One of the first bishops of the North African church during the third century was Cyprian, the bishop of Carthage, a city where I lived for a couple of years. The belief in the reality of demonic powers was widespread in North Africa. Cyprian lived in a world where demonic forces, evil spirits and magic were viewed as real presences to be combated. Cyprian, a famous lawyer, flamboyant rhetorician and wealthy man before his conversion, had been caught up in this spirit world and had acquired a reputation as a wonderworker and magician.

In A.D. 246 Cyprian went through a dramatic conversion experience, finding a miraculous release from the vices that had enslaved him. He describes his experience in these words: "I myself was held in bonds by the innumerable errors of my previous life. . . . But after that, by the help of the waters of new birth . . . a second birth has restored me to a new man."[5] As a bishop he saw many of his ministerial activities as direct and immediate confrontations between the powers of light and darkness.

The modern era of Christianity in Africa was inaugurated by freed slaves. The first missionaries to Africa established settlements both on the coast and in the interior, gathering around themselves small groups who were to be their first converts, most of whom were freed slaves. In many places repatriated or liberated slaves laid the foundations of the present African church. In 1792 the first church was established in Africa by emancipated slaves returning from

America. This is why today you find cities in Africa called Freetown (the capital of Sierra Leone) and Libreville (the capital of Gabon), which was a former naval base against the slave trade.

In today's Africa this emphasis on God's freedom and on Christ the conqueror is more prevalent than ever. This is well illustrated by the version of the Apostles' Creed used by the Masai tribe in Kenya. The section on the resurrection goes: "He lay buried in the grave, but the hyenas did not touch him, and on the third day, he rose from the grave. He ascended to the skies. He is the Lord."[6]

The late Festo Kivengere, a dynamic evangelist and Ugandan Anglican bishop of the diocese of Kigezi, was exiled during Idi Amin's regime. I once heard him ask the question, "What can you preach to the Ugandans who have suffered incomparably and lost everything [due to Amin] and now feel in complete bondage?" His answer was: "The only thing you can preach is the Resurrection. That he whose power overcame the greatest of evil forces can help them overcome." There is no question that the power of the resurrection became the theme of Bishop Festo's life and message.

During a visit to Kampala, the Ugandan capital, I had dinner with Bishop Festo. He told me that when he visited a new town for an evangelistic meeting, he often visited the homes of non-Christians. When the topic of his beliefs came up during their conversation, he told them all about the freedom that Christ had brought to his life. Then he asked them how their god or religion had freed them. More often than not he found that this question stumped them, as they had never thought of their religious life in those terms.

Guinea, in West Africa, is a predominantly Muslim country that has seen only a marginal response to the gospel among the Muslim population. On one of my visits I came across an indigenous independent church that had grown to well over one thousand members in just six months. Most of the expatriates were skeptical of its success, yet not one of those to whom I spoke had actually visited. I took the opportunity of attending one of their services and found that they put a significant emphasis on the dangers of spirits, witchcraft and occult powers. The recurring theme throughout the service was the freedom that God offers Christians.

There is no question that the churches growing most quickly in Africa are those emphasizing the supernatural power of God. Interestingly, most converts from Islamic and animistic backgrounds want to leave all of their previous religious trappings completely because they feel that they have experienced true freedom through the power of God, dramatically breaking away from their past, which they see as bondage. Ironically, it is often today's expatriate Christian workers who find themselves encouraging new converts not to forsake all their religious traditions, helping them to sort out the difference between those traditions that are incompatible with the Christian faith and those that are simply religious and cultural.

It is often in the midst of our times of greatest captivity or bondage that God chooses to display his freedom most clearly. I have met people in Africa who had committed terrible crimes and found themselves in appalling living conditions in one of the notorious African prisons. Right there they had found God revealing himself to them, so that they discovered true freedom of the heart and mind for the first time. Time and time again I have heard refugees and others throughout Africa share similar stories. The Christian good news in Africa is liberation—from the moral and spiritual miseries that Christ came to deliver us from. There is a battle waging between the forces of life and those of death. In the Christian life these two kingdoms rise up against one another—that of heaven and that of this world, of God and of Satan, of life and of death. And within this the growing Christian is increasingly being freed from the forces of darkness.

The Pilgrim's Progress, written from a prison cell by John Bunyan, illustrates this beautifully. One passage finds Christian and

Hopeful locked in the dungeon of Doubting Castle by the Giant
Despair:

> Hopeful says, "Indeed our present condition is dreadful and death
> would be far more welcome to me, than thus forever to abide: But yet
> let us consider, the Lord of the Country to which we are going, hath
> said, . . . others so far as I can understand, have been taken by him, as
> well as we; and yet have escaped out of his hands, who knows . . . the
> time may come to give us a happy release.

Later Christian realizes that the chance of escape is at hand:

> "What a Fool," quoth he, "am I, thus to lie in a stinking dungeon,
> when I may as well walk at liberty? I have a key in my bosom, called
> Promise, that will I am persuaded open any lock in the castle.". . .
> Then Christian pulled it out of his bosom and began to try at the dun-
> geon door, whose bolt (as he turned the key) gave back, and the door
> flew open with ease, and Christian and Hopeful both came out. Then
> he went to the outward door that leads into the castle yard, and with
> his key opened that door also. After he went to the Iron Gate, for that
> must be opened too, but that lock went very hard, yet the key did
> open it. Then they thrust open the gate to make their escape with
> speed. . . . Then they went on and came to the King's Highway again
> and so were safe.[7]

Our "Key of Promise" is that God in his very essence is freedom.
Christ came to set us free in all dimensions of our lives—in different
ways for each of us at the various stages of our Christian lives. And
for the disease within Western Christianity of having a powerless
God comes the cure of African Christianity.

Our Role in God's Freedom

African Christians understand their experience of God's freedom as
a responsibility. They believe that God frees us so we can effectively
live out his plan for us to its fullest extent. To them this plan means
representing his character to others, thus bringing about their free-

dom also. African Christians believe that God frees them so that he can use them to free others. Only those who are themselves first free can carry the good news of freedom to others. The question that African Christians put to us in the West is: "Are you spreading news of the freedom that Christ is and brings?"

The late Hans R. Rookmaaker, an art historian from Amsterdam, said, "Freedom is not just negative, freedom *from* something: on the contrary, freedom opens up possibilities, freedom is *for,* towards something. Christian freedom is positive, dynamic."[8]

Joseph in the Old Testament, a resident in Africa, realized that God continually provided him with freedom in order that he should free others. Genesis says that God sent Joseph to Egypt to "save lives" (Gen 45:5). God had obviously planned Joseph's life all the way through. God's ultimate, long-term purpose was that Joseph should free others, saving the Israelite people and many Egyptians from death by famine.

Joseph's life story—during which he was often liberated, as we saw earlier—is actually also a series of examples of freeing others. He freed his family when they came to Egypt by guaranteeing that they had the best of everything. His presence revived his father Jacob's spirit. He freed both Potiphar and the prison warden through his superb work ethic. In prison he freed Pharaoh's cupbearer and baker from their confusion by interpreting their dreams. He freed Pharaoh by giving him insight and wisdom through the interpretation of his dreams. God used Joseph to free the people of Egypt and the neighboring countries from famine. During the last year of the famine when there was a great lack of food, he freed the Egyptians and Canaanites by giving them food in exchange for their livestock. After his father died his brothers thought he would take revenge on them for having sold him into slavery many years before. He freed them of this fear by taking care of them and providing for their children. Because Joseph had been liberated, he became a liberator.

On one occasion, I arrived at Entebbe Airport in Uganda and was told by a small, elderly customs lady to open up my suitcase for inspection. I opened it, and right on top was a Christian book I was reading entitled *Loving God* by Charles Colson. Noticing the book she looked straight into my eyes and asked, "Do you love God?" I explained that I was a Christian. She then put her hand on my shoulder and asked me, "But do you know the freedom he gives?" For this elderly saint God's freedom was the most important message for her to share.

I have always been moved by Desmond Tutu's pleas and prayers for freedom in South Africa. In an address he gave at St. George's Cathedral in Cape Town in March 1988, he repeatedly prayed for God's freedom for blacks and whites. He believed that neither were free—some were bound by having no rights, others bound by hatred and corruption. This continual Christian emphasis on all peoples of South Africa needing liberation, though in different ways, was one of the key elements of the church's strategic role in South Africa's transformation.

The Central African Republic has lived under some very corrupt regimes, yet it has a solid and strong church. One incident will never allow me to forget Bangui, the country's capital. I was scheduled to arrive at the airport at midnight for a meeting at 9 a.m. My flight was delayed three hours, and by the time I had maneuvered my way through airport immigrations and customs officials, it was 4 a.m. I was met by about six church leaders who drove me to my hotel. I expected that they would drop me off to check in, take a quick shower, have a brief rest and then be picked up for the meeting. Instead we stayed in the car in the hotel parking lot until 8:30 a.m. while they told me enthusiastically, without a break in their conversation, the many ways in which God was providing freedom in their country, in their churches and in their individual lives. They could not contain their joy about the faithfulness of God.

In Africa I once met a man on a plane who had been an engineer.

He had now made it his full-time responsibility and commitment to free children who had been forced into labor as bonded laborers—effectively slaves—and to help them with a new beginning. Devoting all their energies to this cause, he and his colleagues had freed thousands of bonded laborers over the last ten years. It meant some risk—two of his coworkers had been killed. But he said that he believed in Gandhi's philosophy of the last man—that is, that the bonded laborer is the last man in society, and they were there to liberate the last man. What a splendid parallel that is of living out the Christian faith.

The most trapped areas of our lives can bring us closer to God than anything else—once he has freed us. Only then can we come to realize that his gift of freedom is the most precious gift that we can offer to others. The founder of the Taizé Christian community in France, Brother Roger, has worked in Africa and has written a beautiful prayer which speaks of this.

> *Freed*
> O Christ,
> You take upon yourself all our burdens
> so that,
> freed of all that weighs us down,
> we can constantly begin anew to walk
> with lightened step,
> from worry towards trusting
> from the shadows towards the deep flowing waters,
> from our own will
> towards the vision of the coming Kingdom.
> And then we know,
> though we hardly dared hope so,
> that you offer to make every human being
> a reflection of your face.[9]

Dr. Martin Luther King Jr., the African-American minister whose entire life was focused on the freedom of his people, has been widely accepted and treasured by African Christians. The closing words of his historic speech made in Washington, D.C., in 1963 are dearly loved in Africa. However, African Christians relate them not only to civil rights but to the complete spiritual freedom God provides for his children. From that perspective these already powerful words become all the more powerful:

> With this faith we will be able . . . to stand up for freedom together, knowing that we will be free one day. . . . Let freedom ring. . . . And when we allow freedom to ring, when we let it ring from every village and hamlet, from every state and city, we will be able to speed up that day when all of God's children—black men and white men, Jews and Gentiles, Catholics and Protestants—will be able to join hands and sing in the words of the old Negro spiritual, "Free at last, free at last; thank God Almighty, we are free at last."[10]

The Christian life is a long walk to freedom, as Nelson Mandela of South Africa appropriately titled his autobiography. A long walk it may be—but once on the road it becomes an irresistible and joyful journey of liberation.

—6—

Unboxing God

East Asia's Emphasis on the Surprises of God

Rudyard Kipling, the Nobel Prize-winning author of The *Jungle Book,* left India, where he was living in 1889, for a long journey through East Asia. One of the most misinterpreted quotations is Kipling's "East is East and West is West and never the twain shall meet." The traditional understanding of this quotation is that there exists a gulf between the East and West, and one side will never fully understand the other. However, the full verse is as follows:

> Oh, the East is East and the West is West and never the twain shall meet,
> Till Earth and Sky stand presently at God's great judgement seat,
> But there is neither East nor West, border nor breed nor birth
> When two strong men stand face to face, though they come from the ends of the earth.[1]

Kipling wrote this out of his experiences of traveling in the East, and in this context he indicated that there is a common ground where the East and West can know each other. His common ground was in our common humanity. But we, as Western Christians, can have a much stronger common ground with Christians in East Asia by learning from their experience of God's involvement in their lives. I have found this to be true while working in the East.

One day I was walking down the almost impenetrably populous Nathan Road in Kowloon, Hong Kong, when I came across a game focused around ten straw baskets of varying sizes set up on a street corner. About twenty people surrounded the baskets, and on joining the group I soon realized that the "game host" selected an onlooker at random whom he dared to open a basket of his or her choice. This happened several times: each time a person removed the lid with great trepidation—an oversized stuffed animal popped out. Each time this brought great relief to the player. It was like a Chinese form of jack-in-the-box. I was not able to determine, though, why there was so much suspense and fear associated with opening the baskets. Then the game host pointed to me, daring me to open the smallest of the baskets. I accepted the challenge and nonchalantly lifted the lid only to jump back immediately, trembling nervously as the crowd roared with laughter. For as soon as I raised the lid a large cobra sprang up and looked me in the eyes.

East Asia is a region that specializes in the surprises of life. Within this context Christians in East Asia are known for emphasizing the fact that God does not live in a box. Their strongest perception of God is that he cannot be confined, is not limited, that his ways are unpredictable and that he operates through the unexpected. Furthermore, with this view of God their experience is that the outcomes of his workings are always so much better, greater and more perfect than they ever imagined. It is in this way that Christianity has interacted with East Asian culture for many centuries.

John the Baptist—A Misunderstanding of Jesus' Way

John the Baptist, Jesus' cousin and the one who prepared the way for him, went through an experience that entirely stretched his understanding of the way Jesus worked. Matthew wrote of an incident at the end of John's life, when John found himself in prison, in the dungeons of the fortress of Machaerus in the mountains east of the Dead Sea (Mt 11:1-11).

He had been imprisoned by the ruler, Herod Antipas of Galilee, because he had spoken out publicly against Herod's behavior in seducing his brother's wife and marrying her. When John had been in prison about seven months, he began to hear reports of Jesus' ministry from his own disciples. Events were happening so differently from how he expected that he felt confused and even disillusioned and seriously questioned Jesus and the way he was choosing to work.

After all, John had given his whole life to preparing for Christ's coming and ministry, and now he was sitting in prison while at the same time Jesus' ministry was taking on an appearance wholly different from what he had foreseen. So he sent his disciples to Jesus to ask: "Are you the one who was to come, or should we expect someone else?"

In many ways it seems unbelievable that this man who had baptized Jesus and said, "Look, the Lamb of God who takes away the sins of the world" (Jn 1:29), is now doubting. It is important to remember, however, that John's entire message had been one of judgment—that the Messiah would come to judge the unrighteous. There was very little compassion in its content. Additionally, he probably imagined like so many others that the Messiah would come with physical and military force to overthrow Roman rule. He expected the messianic kingdom to be ushered in cataclysmically, suddenly. Many Jews at the time believed the Messiah, God's anointed king, would be a great superhuman figure dashing into history to remake the world and vindicate the Jews. Their Messiah would have been the most destructive conqueror in history, smashing his enemies into utter extinction. Now, stuck in prison, John was beginning to realize that Jesus was not planning anything of the kind.

Jesus totally surprised him with the answer to his question. John may have expected, or inwardly hoped, that Jesus would say something like, "My armies are gathering. Caesarea, the Roman headquarters, is about to fall. Judgment is beginning." Instead, Jesus told John's disciples, "Go back and report to John what you hear and see: The blind receive sight, the lame walk, those who have leprosy are cured, the deaf hear, the dead are raised, and the good news is preached to the poor" (Mt 11:4-5). Jesus is actually quoting a prophetic prediction about the Messiah found in the Old Testament book of Isaiah (Is 61:1).

The irony here is that this same passage was the basis for John's entire ministry. It was one that he knew backward and forward—a passage that said the Messiah's divine accreditation would be his miracles and his concern for the poor. While knowing the text well, however, John had misunderstood the whole foundation on which Jesus' mission was being built. Jesus in effect says to John, "Maybe I am not doing the things you expected me to do, but the powers of evil are being defeated in another way, my way, a better way."

God Is Bigger Than Our Perceptions

Both the story of John the Baptist and the experiences of Christians throughout East Asia remind us that God is not limited or restrained by our finite perceptions of him and of how he can work. East Asian Christians have a very big view of God.

In the West we often separate our understanding of God's character from the ways in which we expect him to display himself. We often have preconceived views as to how God operates such as, "He works in this or that way today," or "He does not work like this today," or "He reveals himself in this or that way," or "He does not reveal himself in that way." The Chinese have a unique concept of change and relativity called the *Yin* and *Yang*. It is a way of "both/ and" thinking that includes the possibility of either/or. The Yin and Yang mindset believes that opposites are in harmony. The word "and" is the "Holy Conjunction." Rather than an either/or perspective, the East Asians emphasize both/and thinking. The story is told about the professor who was asked by one of his students, "Sir, it is said you believe that at the core of all truth is paradox. Is that correct?" "Well," the professor answered, "yes and no."

Christians in East Asia bring this Yin/Yang worldview into their Christian faith. In thinking paradoxically they do not put restrictions on God or put him in a box. Every time I have visited countries in East Asia, I have been told about and have experienced remarkable and awe-inspiring displays of God's workings. Yet each time, while I would stand in sheer amazement and at times disbelief, the local Christians almost expected it as the norm of their Christian life-experience. Westerners, living in an "Age of Reason," try to analyze such happenings, while in East Asia, Christians expect God to work in unexplainable and paradoxical ways and are not given to an analytical faith.

A unique perspective on the Chinese and East Asian worldview and mindset is gained by studying the contrasts between Chinese art and architecture and those of the West. Chinese art attempts to inspire rapt contemplation of the natural world, hence the predominance of landscapes in Chinese paintings. However, Chinese landscape painting is different from most Western landscape art in that it is not focused on human vision and anthropocentric space; rather, it is concerned with the endlessness of nature. Their paintings are not intended to ue realistic but rather contemplative—which is why in Chinese landscapes you often see mountains covered in heavy mist or clouds. This lack of definition leads you to reflect or speculate further. As far as Chinese painting is concerned, the Western necessity of an "enclosing frame" is a contradiction in terms.

In China during the Southern Ch'i dynasty (A.D. 479–501), the Emperor commissioned the artist Hsieh Ho to write *The Six Canons of Painting,* which are highly esteemed by Chinese artists to this day. Interestingly, none of the rules given restrict or limit the artist. Rather they are concerned with giving significance and spontaneity to painting and reducing the restrictions. The first canon is the most important because it requires the painter to reveal the ch'i, the "Breadth of Heaven," in the work of his brush. These six canons defy the definitive translation of realism in Chinese painting.

Choan-Seng Song, an Asian theologian, has said that Christians "who are not endowed with [Western] eyes should not be prevented from seeing Christ differently. They must train themselves to see Christ through Chinese eyes, Japanese eyes." He offers as an example a painting, *The Cross of Christ,* by the Japanese Christian artist Giichro Hayakawa, saying, "The whole picture is a paragon of tranquillity in the midst of a raging storm." He calls it a *sibui* Christ— sibui describing a quality that "conveys a controlled reserve toward life and the world." Sibui is "eloquent in silence, aggressive in reservation, forceful in reserve. It is a sibui Christ that we encounter here. . . . Is this not a sibui spirituality that is seen in the Saviour of the world?"[2] Once again the interpenetration of opposites, which leads to unpredictability, is seen as characteristic of how Jesus displayed himself, indicating a boundless view of God.

Chinese architecture is equally all-encompassing in structure. The uniquely designed pagodas—the sacred religious buildings in China—illustrate this worldview. Pagodas are composed of geometric tiers, with each level narrowing up to the top of the structure. When a Westerner looks at a pagoda, he or she usually begins at the base and looks upward. However, the Chinese, I have been told, begin at the top and look downward, seeing the tiers enlarge rather than diminish in size.

Next to the Bible and the Bhagavad-Gita, the Tao Te Ching, or "Book of the Way," is the most translated book in the world. It is the sacred book of religious Taoism, written by the Chinese philosopher Lao-tzu in 604 B.C. Taoism subscribes to the notion that there is a single, overarching "Way" that encompasses everything in the universe. It is the centerpiece of all Chinese religion and thought. The Tao Te Ching is very ambiguous in its content, so much so that it is very difficult to understand. The text even says something to the effect that if you understand these words then you do not understand them. An example of its nonrestrictive, paradoxical view of life is seen in the following verses:

> The Way is gained by daily loss, loss upon loss, until at last comes rest. By letting go, it all gets done; the world is won by those who let it go.
>
> Who knows the reason for Heaven's likes? The Way of Heaven does not war yet is good at conquering, does not speak, yet is good at answering, is not summoned, yet comes of itself, is relaxed, yet good at making life plans. Heaven's net is vast; though its meshes are wide, nothing escapes.[3]

Culturally and historically the Chinese and East Asian mindset is a nonrestrictive one. People do not seek to put limitations on things but instead are always attempting to remove the restrictions.

Christians in East Asia bring this nonrestrictive mindset to their faith and therefore all the more expect God to be like that in the way he operates. This large view of God freely allows him to work unboxed in their lives. The faith of East Asian Christians is bound up closely with the way they see the world—their family life, their sense of identity, even their national histories. They do not separate their Christianity from their social, political, economic and personal lives. It is all intertwined.

In much of Asia rural lifestyles prevail. And when you meet

Christians in rural areas, it is very evident that their faith pervades all facets of their lives, from their families to the outcome of their harvests. The Japanese Christian writer Kosuké Koyama wrote of a "three-mile-an-hour God," who travels at the walking pace of Asian villagers, meeting them wherever they are.

It certainly stretched my own faith to see East Asian Christians unboxing God. Once in the Philippine capital, Manila, I saw a Christian group distributing leaflets and tracts in the streets, and I asked my Filipino host how effective this was in communicating the Christian faith. While acknowledging that many of the leaflets got thrown away, he went on to share his own story with me. About ten years earlier while he was at university, someone had given him a tract in the street that he promptly put in a book he was carrying. At that time, as far as he was concerned, that tract was completely irrelevant. For some reason he never finished reading that book. Seven years later, seeing it on his shelves, he decided to finish reading it. He was at a very low ebb, suffering from depression and deep loneliness, and had thought of taking his life. On opening the book he found the tract, faded and looking out-of-date, but speaking exactly to the specific difficult situation in his life at that moment. He went to the church whose address was on the tract, and the eventual result was that he became a Christian. When I met him, he was a leader in a Filipino Christian organization. He had noted my skepticism at the effectiveness of tract distribution, and he was wisely cautioning me never to be closed-minded about how God can and does work.

Time and time again in the various encounters I have had with Christians in East Asia, I have been reminded that they expect the unexpected. As far as they are concerned, God is a God of surprises. They actually find a sense of peace and calm at not knowing at all how God will work in a particular situation.

Throughout the Bible we find example after example of men and women who unboxed God by not putting limitations on him, by choosing to believe in the extraordinary—from Joshua's experience of the sun standing still, to Gideon's amazing victory using just lanterns and trumpets, to Esther's crucial role in the salvation of her people in Persia. The countless stories in both the Old and New Testaments of individuals who chose to allow God to work unrestrained in their lives are perhaps best affirmed in the Lord's words in Isaiah 55:8-9: "My thoughts are not your thoughts, neither are my ways your ways. . . . As the heavens are higher than the earth, so are my ways higher than your ways, and my thoughts than your thoughts."

A key figure in the history of Christianity in Asia is the early nineteenth-century English missionary William Carey. The favorite and repeated topic of many of Carey's addresses was the need for us to stretch our perceptions of God and his actions. Isaiah 54:2 was his theme-text: "Enlarge the place of your tent, stretch your tent curtains wide, do not hold back; lengthen your cords, strengthen your stakes." East Asian Christianity encourages us to take every opportunity to enlarge our own view of God.

God Is Greater Than Our Circumstances

Not only is God bigger than our perceptions of him, he is equally greater than the difficult situations in which we may find ourselves—nor is he limited by them. John the Baptist, by the time he was put in prison, was a household name to the Jews and to many Romans in Palestine. He was known as the one whose very existence entailed preparing the way for Jesus and proclaiming that he was indeed the Messiah. He was intimately identified with Jesus. And yet, once he was in prison, we find him doubting Jesus' identity.

Matthew's Gospel provides some unique insights into John's thoughts during his prison crisis (Mt 11:1-11). It is interesting to observe that it was while Jesus' twelve disciples were away on their first mission that John seized the moment to send his own disciples to question Jesus. John did not want anyone to know his questions and doubts, especially as some of Jesus' disciples such as Andrew and Philip were formerly his disciples. So John got his disciples to approach Jesus when he was alone, in secret.

He told his disciples to ask Jesus: "Are you the one who was to come?" Interestingly, the "one to come" was not a recognized Messianic title in Judaism—perhaps indicating that John was not committing himself but was leaving open the possibility that Jesus might not be the Messiah.

Obviously John was very discouraged to have come to this point in his thinking, after having proclaimed Jesus as being the Messiah for so long. It is helpful to note that John in effect is the last of the Old Testament prophets, those under the order of the law. Jesus was bringing in a new order, one of grace. So in this regard John had a transitional role. And transition bred insecurity—he did not see how he fitted into the new scheme. His unique role had ceased to exist. Yet in the midst of the most difficult situation in John's life, Jesus reassured him that what was to come was better than anything he could ever envision or predict.

East Asian culture thrives on the unpredictable. *The Story of the Stone,* considered to be the greatest Chinese novel, was written by Cao Xuequin and Kao Ou in the mid-1700s. It is extremely complex, with over four hundred characters. One of the book's primary characteristics, which makes it so engrossing to read, is that it focuses on the unpredictable. Pao-yu, the central character, repeatedly finds himself in trouble and in very difficult circumstances—the most unimaginable things come to save him, from a mysterious monk to a jade stone.

Like *The Story of the Stone,* the story of God often finds him working in his children's lives in ways that are entirely unanticipated. Yet his ways are always much higher and more purposeful than we could ever dream possible.

On one visit to China I met a Hong Kong resident who had been involved in providing Scriptures to churches throughout China for many years. He told me of an incident when it had been arranged for him to take some Bibles into China. These Scriptures were for a group of pastors in one of the northern provinces of the country who had planned to come south and meet him in the city of Guangzhou (Canton) at a prearranged place. He was able to fit just over a hundred Bibles into his suitcases, discreetly packed to avoid attracting attention. But when he crossed the border, customs officials on the Chinese side searched his bags thoroughly, and all the Bibles were discovered and confiscated. He was still allowed to enter into the country, however.

He checked into his hotel in Guangzhou very discouraged, knowing that the next day he would have to meet these pastors who had traveled for several days to obtain these Scriptures. Late that night there was a knock on his door. Opening it he found a European couple outside who asked if they could talk. They told him that they were Christians and had been behind him in the line at the customs checkpoint. They had seen the confiscation of his Bibles, and it so happened that they also had filled their bags with Bibles, but the customs officials had not searched them. They had checked into their hotel only to receive a message that the person for whom their Bibles were intended was not able to come. To their surprise they then discovered that they were staying in the same hotel as my Hong Kong acquaintance. While having dinner in the hotel restaurant that night they saw him and followed him to his room. Their story finished, they asked if he knew someone who could use the two hundred Bibles they had in their suitcases.

As this story illustrates, God is not limited by the situations in which we find ourselves, nor is he limited by us. I have often met Christians who at one time believed that God had a special purpose for their lives. However, either through circumstances that did not turn out as expected or after looking at their failures and weaknesses, they gradually gave up hope that God still had a special interest in them. The result was that they began to feel as if they were doomed to second best, not only in life but in terms of their relationship with God.

However, we just need to look at Jesus' dealing with John the Baptist to realize that God does not intend us, no matter what our weaknesses, failures or circumstances, to have to settle for less than his best. John the Baptist in questioning Jesus did the worst thing he could have done—he doubted Jesus' authenticity. Yet Jesus turned around and gave John the greatest compliment of all, saying, "Among those born of women there has not risen anyone greater than John the Baptist" (Mt 11:11).

When in the Philippines I met a seventeen-year-old man named Abbas who was playing a key role in a very successful charity focusing on the thousands of street children in Manila. He had grown up in a Muslim tribe on the Philippine island of Mindanao. When he was thirteen, his parents divorced and began to fight over him, so he ran away. He washed dishes on a boat to pay for the journey from Mindanao to Manila. Not having any family or friends in the city, he quickly ended up on the streets, sniffing glue and stealing to survive. Eventually he was forced into male prostitution. One day in utter desperation he cried out, "God help me, send someone to help me!" A few days later he met someone from the street ministry with which he now works, who took him to their boys' home where he began the process of rehabilitation. Now here he was, a committed Christian, working with all his strength to rescue other children on the streets. To many in Manila, street children are a social embarrassment, mere scum. Consequently, these children are living tragedies, and humanly speaking, you cannot see much hope for them. Yet late one night as I stood among dozens of street children talking to Abbas about their fate, he said an unforgettable thing: "I don't see them as they are, but as how beautiful they can be with God's help."

Megan Gabriel Lanham was a Christian professor of English in China for a number of years until the Tiananmen Square massacre of 1989 in Beijing forced her to leave due to the political tensions. She lived there with her husband, Johnny, their baby and her friend Cari. She records her experiences from this time in her book *Snatched from the Dragon.*

Every week they had an informal evening get-together in the college cafeteria for the Chinese students to practice their English. On one such evening Megan and Cari took Easter eggs along to illustrate the Western Christian holiday of Easter. That evening almost fifty students were gathered around the cafeteria tables as Cari displayed the Easter eggs and explained what the Easter holiday means to Westerners. As Cari spoke, Megan looked for anyone from the college administration who might be monitoring the event for "anti-communist propaganda." Speaking of a Western holiday was safe fare, but speaking of Jesus Christ publicly in such a setting would get them a plane ticket home.

Cari waved one of the Easter eggs: "It reminds us of new life," she was saying. "Think of when the egg cracks and the tiny new life inside stumbles out. That's why we use the egg as a symbol of Easter. Because that's what Christians believe Jesus gives us, as well. New life. And new hope."

Just as Cari said this, they noticed Li Mei, the college's communist informant, standing at the back of the room. Cari fumbled for a split second and then lurched into a different gear. Suddenly one of the students, a young man, darted between the tables toward Li Mei and whispered in her ear. Li Mei nodded with a serious look on her face. Megan's heart pounded, and she closed her eyes, fearing that they would be kicked out of the country.

When Megan opened her eyes, Li Mei was standing next to Cari, talking and gesturing aggressively. It seemed to be just as Megan had feared. Then Cari walked over to Megan to explain what Li Mei had said.

> Megan swallowed hard. "Don't spare me. I can handle it."
> "She said she didn't think the students understood."
> "So when do we have to leave?"
> "Megan, are you listening? Li Mei said the students didn't understand!"
> I blinked twice. "Understand what?"
> "She said we weren't clear enough. The students have questions."
> "About what? Are we on the same subject here?"
> "About Easter, Megan. Li Mei asked us to explain some more about Easter!"
> "She what? And what did you say?"
> Cari grinned a face-splitting grin for such a petite woman.
> "I said, 'Well, if you insist.'"

They immediately reopened the meeting for questions about Easter. One young man wanted to know why Jesus died. And there were many more questions, so many that the meeting ran a half-hour overtime. Megan left the building that night overwhelmed: "Walking home under winter stars, I felt as if I could touch the moon, grab a star, dance with the angels across the cold, black sky. I felt that close to God."[4]

That was just one night's informal English language session. The following night they showed a video on the life of Christ. And amazingly, at the end of the week, one of the students was baptized.

God is looking for individuals who, even in the midst of their difficult circumstances, continue to believe in his good purposes and allow him to work as he wishes in their lives. Christians throughout East Asia, in the living out of their Christian faith, strongly confirm that God does not live in a box and that he is not

limited either by our perceptions of him or by any of the circumstances of our lives. Their challenge to Western Christians is to
keep enlarging our view of God by allowing him to work unboxed
in our lives.

—7—

Expatriates, Spiritually Speaking

Our Common "Crosscultural" Identity

T*hinking about Christians in other countries and cultures* raises the question of our own identity as well. It is certainly true that the richness of living among Christians of other nationalities, within their respective cultures, cannot be overvalued. These opportunities of learning from other cultural expressions of the Christian faith are unique and beautiful windows on God and the displaying of his character. However, many of us in the West never have the opportunity to live as foreigners in other countries. The closest we come to reaping the spiritual benefits of being in another cultural setting is through contact with the ever increasing number of foreigners living among us, in our own churches and communities. Nevertheless, no matter where we live, from a spiritual viewpoint all of us as Christians are foreigners, exiles from our true home.

It is hard to understand the full ramifications of being a foreigner until you have lived in another cultural environment. There are numerous frustrations simply because as a foreigner you do not know the way systems work locally. While living abroad I have spent hours waiting in lines to pay a telephone bill, obtain a residence visa or register a car (among many other reasons), only to find when getting to the front that I had been in the wrong line, or that I did not need to be in the line at all, or that there was a shortcut to the front used by nationals to avoid the wait. Immense frustration and loss of time resulted simply from a lack of the local savoir-faire. Many frustrations and hassles result simply from being a foreigner. Ask a Palestinian or Sudanese refugee about what it is like being a foreigner—they have a wealth of stories about the discomforts and difficulties of being an alien.

Life as a foreigner can also give rise to humorous or even embarrassing situations. The official European Community translators have gathered dozens of examples of incorrect usage of English in non-English-speaking countries. Take the Paris hotel that told its guests, "Please leave your values at the desk." An Acapulco hotel reassured guests about the drinking water by saying, "The manager has personally passed all the water served here." A notice in a Norwegian cocktail lounge stated, "Ladies are requested not to have children in the bar." A Rome doctor specialized in "Women and other diseases"—and for people suffering toothache in Hong Kong, a dentist advertised tooth extraction "using the latest Methodists." A sign in a Budapest zoo showed the difficulties in Eastern Europe: "Please do not feed the animals. If you have any suitable food, give it to the guard on duty." And if you thought flying was fun, go to Copenhagen Airport where one airline vowed to "take your bags and send them in all directions."

A British policeman at Heathrow Airport told me of a humorous incident involving the Albanian national football team. The Albanian team and its coaches, thirty-seven people in all, once passed through Heathrow in transit to another country. As they did not speak English well, they misunderstood the "Duty Free" signs and thought they meant "All Free." And all thirty-seven of them entered the duty-free shops and began filling their bags and pockets with items of their choice. They then walked out nonchalantly past the cashier. The airport police were summoned to arrest them, but after twenty-four hours they released them from jail in frustration, as they could not find anyone who could speak Albanian to serve as a translator.

For most of my life I have been an expatriate. More often than not I have lived as a foreigner in countries other than my own. To many, expatriate living conjures up thoughts of adventure, exotic cuisine, learning about a foreign culture, different climates, new languages, crosscultural friendships and a continual state of touristic sightseeing. On one hand, living in a different country can be all of these and more. On the other hand, living in an unfamiliar environment to which you do not truly and completely belong can eventually result in a good deal of stress, tension and pressure. These frustrations can build to the point where they no longer seem bearable. As I have frequently seen, the reaction is often for the expatriate to want to run away, to escape from it all, to go home.

M. Scott Peck begins his bestselling book *The Road Less Traveled:* "Life is difficult." At times, pain or suffering or discouragement make us wish we could just run away, to get out of the place or situation bringing us so much hardship. At one time or another almost everyone has experienced these feelings to some extent. On one occasion I was involved in organizing an extensive Scripture distribution program in Moscow, with numerous events—including concerts at the Kremlin. The Russian coordinator for the entire program could no longer handle the pressure and simply left the country to attend a conference in Hungary, literally hours before the program began.

I happened to be in Zaire over the Christmas season in 1986. With many speaking engagements ahead of me in a language I had not used for some time, I came down with pericarditis, an infection around my heart. I vividly remember sitting on the wrought-iron bed in my room, all alone, in pain, and having the distinct thought that I wanted to run away. The words of one of the Psalms described my feelings exactly when feeling overwhelmed: "Oh that I had the wings of a dove! I would fly away and be at rest—I would flee far away and stay in the desert. I would hurry to my place of shelter, far from the tempest and storm" (Ps 55:6).

The Flight of Elijah

It is often easy to put biblical characters on pedestals, especially the Old Testament prophets who can seem completely other-worldly in their orientation. The prophet Elijah, perhaps more than any other prophet, miraculously displayed God's power. We can find it difficult to identify with him.

In 1 Kings, however, we find him in a situation that had brought him right down to earth, a period when he longed to run away. Before the crisis developed, he went through a series of intense supernatural experiences that were not only dramatic but also emotionally draining. First, he proclaimed a nationwide drought. His own needs were met by food brought by ravens sent from God. Following this he took a widow's meager amount of flour and oil and extended them miraculously to feed her whole family. Later he went on to raise the widow's son from the dead. These events climaxed with the monumental confrontation on Mount Carmel between Elijah and the 450 prophets of Baal and 400 prophets of Asherah. The confrontation centered around two altars, one his and one theirs, with a bull on each, and the 850 prophets calling on their gods to send fire. When they received no response, Elijah dramatically poured water over his altar and called on God, who responded by sending so much fire that it completely burned up even the stone altar.

After all these events, with the last being an issue of life or death, Elijah was so emotionally exhausted that he ran away from the evil Queen Jezebel, even though she had lost all her power and allies. First he took flight into the desert (1 Kings 19:4). His whole life had been a struggle against Baal worship, and he could not go on any longer, so he prayed to die: "I have had enough, LORD. . . . Take my life." He fell asleep, perhaps to escape from it all. When he awoke, still in deep discouragement, he felt such a desperate need for God's help that he set out on a journey of nearly 480 kilometers to Mount Horeb, a place of God's unique historic presence, the place where Moses had received his commission to lead the Israelites out of Egypt.

Elijah's state of desperation was partly due to the issue of identity. He felt like a foreigner, an alien, a stranger when he said, "I am the only one left" (1 Kings 19:10), thinking he was the sole remaining prophet faithful to the Lord God. The consequences of feeling like a foreigner, a complete outsider, were finally too much for him.

Christians as Foreigners

The picture of Christians as aliens, foreigners or temporary residents is a constant theme throughout the New Testament. One of the difficulties in understanding the Scriptures today is that our world is very different from the world in New Testament times—it no longer contains the circumstances from which some figures of speech were drawn. There are times when we do not grasp the full force of the language used in the Bible because our perception is so different from that of the writer.

The terms "strangers," "foreigners" and "aliens" are figures of speech from the rules and terminology of Roman law, defining the legal distinctions between Roman citizens and noncitizens. Both the apostle

Peter in his writings and the writer of Hebrews used the idea of the alien as a metaphor of the Christian life. More specifically they emphasized that a Christian is a foreigner, or expatriate, in this present world. Peter, for example, states that we are "strangers in the world" (1 Pet 1:1), and elsewhere he begins his writing by saying, "I urge you as aliens and strangers in the world" (1 Pet 2:11).

To the original Palestinian readers, strangers and foreigners meant the Gentiles—the non-Jews, the ritually unclean. The Samaritan woman at the well was shocked that Jesus, a Jew, would even talk to her. Within the religious tradition of the Jews there was an ingrained concept of the "otherness" of the stranger, the fact that he or she did not belong.

The Roman readers of the Epistles had an equally sharp sense of the force of the words. Most of the inhabitants of the Roman empire were officially classified as "aliens" in two categories. First, there were those who lived in a territory that was part of the Roman Empire; second, there were those who lived in territories allied to Rome. Complete outsiders who did not belong in either of these categories were treated as hostile and likely to be enslaved.

All aliens were considered "subjects" of Rome rather than citizens. Consequently, they were not fully integrated into the Roman community and could not feel at home within that environment. The disadvantages of being an alien, compared to the advantages of Roman citizenship, were numerous.

The writer of Hebrews, using this political situation as his analogy, makes it very clear that Christians are not really at home in this world, for at their deepest level of being they are looking for another (Heb 11:9-16). He first wrote about Abraham, whose faith looked beyond this world. When Abraham was wandering in Palestine, his mind and thoughts were often at home with God. And it was Abraham's knowledge of his true citizenship that helped him face the difficulties and discouragements of his life. Even when living in the desert this remembrance of his true home helped him maintain perspective. However, there were still times when he wanted to run away, like the day when he faced King Abimelech after having lied about his wife's identity.

The writer of Hebrews uses several Greek terms to describe the patriarchs of the Old Testament, like Abraham—those "unforgettable fathers." They are called "strangers" *(xenoi)*. In the ancient world the fate of a stranger was very hard, as he or she was always regarded with contempt, suspicion and hatred (Heb 11:13). In Sparta in ancient Greece for example a stranger *(xenos)* was often synonymous with a barbarian. At that time when social clubs had their common meal, people divided their members into "members" and "strangers."

Abraham was also called a "sojourner" *(paroikos)*. A sojourner, or a resident alien, was what the Jews were called when they were captives in Babylon and Egypt. Sojourners were not much above a slave in the social scale—they were outsiders, and only on financial payment could they become members of the community.

The third term used for the patriarchs in Hebrews 11 is "foreigner" *(parepidēmos)*, meaning a person who was staying temporarily and who had his or her permanent home somewhere else. During the New Testament period it was considered a humiliating thing to be a foreigner because it usually meant that you had been forced to leave your home country, and this was viewed as a curse from God.

The writer of Hebrews used the example of the patriarchs to encourage his audience not to give up or run away from situations. For the patriarchs never lost their ultimate vision or hope, never gave up the journey and never turned back, because they were "looking forward to the city with foundations, whose architect and builder is God" (Heb 11:10)—the city of the living God.

It is often difficult to be in places where you are a foreigner. In

many ways you are more vulnerable because you do not completely
fit into the local culture and community. When I was seriously ill in
Zaire, I had to return home sooner than had been planned. As I was
still very sick and weak, I decided to go through the airport customs
and immigration point to the departure lounge much earlier than
everyone else. As no one else was around, however, the Zairian customs soldiers chose to hassle and taunt me at gunpoint to the point
of threatening to take all my belongings, including the clothes I was
wearing. At another time I found myself lost in a city in China. I did
not speak Chinese and could not communicate with anyone. Besides
that, I did not have the name and address of my hotel with me. There
were no taxis, just thousands of people riding bicycles, and I did not
have any money with me. I had absolutely no idea where I was or
where to go. When the first bus came by, I got on, hoping it would
take me to a familiar place. The whole experience left me feeling
very vulnerable.

An American I know well was caught outside by soldiers after a
curfew imposed by a new government following a coup d'état in
Liberia. He was forced at gunpoint to take off his shirt and "swim"
on the ground across the asphalt street that he had been crossing.
Foreigners are most definitely in a position of greater vulnerability,
as they are away from the familiarities and securities of home.

Some of the early Christians of North Africa, where I lived as an
expatriate, spoke and wrote extensively on this theme. Tertullian of
Carthage said of a Christian, "He knows that on earth he has a pilgrimage . . . that his dignity is in heaven." During the early fifth century Augustine, bishop of Hippo, emphasized in one of his sermons
that "we are sojourners exiled from our Fatherland." For Christians
this world is not fully our home, and therefore at times when life's
difficulties overwhelm us we may want to run away to our true
home—to God to whom we fully belong, where we can be at peace.

For centuries thinkers have been fascinated by ideas of how to make a better world for people. From Plato until today, people have been writing about what this "other world"—or "Utopia," as Sir Thomas More titled his book in the early 1500s—would be like. Voltaire's short novel *Candide* is a classic example. Candide, a young man who was taught that this is the best of all possible worlds, traveled the world searching for proof. On his journey he faced many hardships and pains, and he discovered the horrors of war. He lived through an earthquake in Lisbon, was flogged by officers of the Inquisition and lost the love of his life. He also discovered wealth only to lose it. However, Candide then visited the famed lost city of the New World, Eldorado, and it changed his life. Eldorado was a utopia with no suffering, poverty or greed. Once having seen this, he knew that his own world was second-best. For in reality there was another place, a better place. And he was never the same again.

I have always been fascinated by both the person and art of Vincent van Gogh. Van Gogh grew up the son of a Protestant Dutch minister and eventually studied evangelism at a Bible institute in Brussels. He went on to serve as a pastor to coal miners in Belgium, until the time came when he was rejected by the church's denominational authorities for his intense identification with the local residents of the mining village. As a result of this rejection he chose for the rest of his life to focus on God's gift to him of art.

Throughout his life van Gogh felt like a stranger in this world. As an artist he was viewed as a failure during his lifetime. He was rejected by his closest friends and felt that he could only relate to his older brother Theo. Van Gogh's whole life was that of an outsider, searching for the city to come. His search for this "other world" was interspersed with glimpses of it portrayed in the vivid, bright colors and the emotion of spiritual victory in his many paintings. Within his desire to run from his difficult life, there were frequent passionate references to God and his character throughout Vincent's numerous letters, most of which were written to Theo.

In his *Self-Portrait,* painted in 1889 while he was in a mental asylum, the period of desperation through which he had passed is evident. The brush strokes are curved (they previously were not), and there is a vibrant intensity throughout the painting. It was obviously painted in a mood of self-confidence and hope, as he painted himself in deep, rich colors. In this painting we see his triumph over sorrow. While in the asylum, after his first emotional breakdown, he painted three paintings of biblical events: *The Good Samaritan, The Resurrection of Lazarus,* and *The Pietà.* Each painting depicts an individual in extreme pain being delivered from his suffering. Identifying with the sufferer, van Gogh painted his own face on these figures. Yet they are not paintings of despair but of hope. For each shows the sufferer being saved by a Savior.

Fundamental to New Testament Christianity is the view that life is an interlude within eternity. This does not in any way mean that as Christians we should detach ourselves from thoroughly integrating into this world. On the contrary, because we know we have another home, we are released as no one else to be deeply involved in this world, not as separatists but as partners and infiltrators. The positive advantage of being foreigners is that we can enjoy all the privileges and freedoms that this status provides—for as foreigners we are cared for and protected by our home country's embassy. The local situation, even when turbulent, does not affect us in the same way it does the nationals.

No matter how deep our integration and involvement in society and life, however, we remain a different type of resident because our hearts are not totally at home. We are a people on the move toward a destination of full belonging. No matter how well we speak the local language, we will always have an accent that gives away our identity—the fact that we are from another place.

Christians as Citizens

While the New Testament uses the metaphors of aliens, strangers and foreigners to describe a Christian's status, it is important to understand that this is only one aspect of our identity.

When Elijah tried to run away because of the loneliness of his situation, the Lord reminded him that there were in fact seven thousand others who had not bowed to Baal (1 Kings 19:14-18). In other words, the Lord was telling Elijah that he did belong somewhere, he was one of the faithful, a citizen of another kingdom.

As Christians we are passport-holders of the greatest country of all. We are full-blooded citizens, in the truest sense, of the City of God. Of all the known New Testament writers the apostle Paul is the only one who writes of the Christian's citizenship. This could well have been because Paul himself was a Roman citizen, with good reason to know the importance of his status and the difference it made not being an alien.

The Roman citizen was one of the privileged class. In this sense Paul was a member of the elite society of his time. Roman citizenship either was obtained by birth or could be bought or given to an individual as an act of grace. Roman citizens could hold political office and responsibility, inherit property and have access to Roman law in terms of commerce and property, with the right to own, buy or sell. They could freely travel throughout the Empire, being protected everywhere by Roman law.

It is in this context that Paul emphasizes the meaning of citizenship in God's kingdom. In his letter to Christians in Philippi he writes, "our citizenship is in heaven" (Phil 3:20). In this sense our home state will protect us and our interests and will intervene on our behalf. Our real home is in heaven, and during this life we are a colony of heaven's citizens.

The metaphor of citizenship was very relevant to the Philippian Christians. Philippi was a Roman military colony in what is today Greece, and most of the residents were Roman soldiers, descendants of veterans of Octavian's and Antony's armies, who were given citizenship as a reward for twenty-one years of military service and settled there on retirement. Philippi was therefore very Roman in orientation—Latin-speaking, with Roman dress styles, Roman magistrates executing Roman justice and morality. The Philippians were resident aliens living in a foreign land, with their citizenship elsewhere. And Paul in effect says to them, "Just as Roman colonists never forget that they belong to Rome, you must never forget that you are citizens of heaven."

The character Christian in *The Pilgrim's Progress* never forgot his identity and his ultimate destination. Christian set out for the Celestial City by heading toward the light in the distance. On his way he faced the Slough of Despond, the Valley of Humiliation, the Valley of the Shadow of Death, Vanity Fair, Doubting Castle and the Valley of Conceit. Finally he came to the River of Death, struggled his way through it and went up the hill to the Celestial City. Christian was someone who continued on his journey by keeping his eyes and mind on his true home, the Celestial City. Throughout the book, he said again and again, "I am on my way to the Celestial City."

Augustine entitled his greatest work *The City of God.* As far as Augustine was concerned, the City of God consists of all those whose end is God and whose home is heaven. In this classic work he wrote: "Now let us hear, let us hear and sing; let us pine for the City where we are citizens. By pining we are already there; we have already cast our hope, like an anchor on that coast."

As Christians we are fully paid-up members of another place, which in this life makes that other place our city of refuge in times of difficulty and need. In the Old Testament Moses appointed six cities, three on each side of the River Jordan, to be cities of refuge. They were to be sanctuaries for those on the run. When the troubles of life make us want to run, the knowledge and remembrance of our citizenship in the City of God can provide our deepest hope and encouragement.

In November 1991 my wife, Lynne, and I attended the largest

church in the city of Bamako in Mali, West Africa. After many "Bonjours" in this French-speaking church we sat down on a bench under a fan, and to our surprise an English-speaking African woman and her little boy joined us. We asked her where she was from, and she answered in a faltering voice that she was a refugee from Liberia and had arrived only one week earlier. Her name was Kahoua, and she went on to tell us her tragic story.

Kahoua had obviously been through deep trauma and still cried as she told of the tragedy. She had lost everything during the uprising in Liberia; her husband, her mother and her father had been killed. Her other child had been taken away, and she had not seen him since. Only she and her son Henry had survived. Her father had been in a government position and was killed when he was on his way to warn his family of the uprising. Severe bloodshed followed, destroying Kahoua's entire village, and she was shot in the leg trying to escape. As she showed us her wound, she continued to tell of how she and her son had been captured. The rebels had taken Henry from her and put her in a locked room, slapped her around and told her they would be back to kill her at 10 p.m. Kahoua began to cry out to the Lord. As she recited Psalm 23, her leg still bleeding from the bullet wound, having lost her whole family and now with her son's life in danger as well, she said she knew the presence of God was with her. The soldier who had threatened her returned abruptly, dragging another woman along with him. He and several other soldiers stripped the other woman and cut her with a knife; while they were distracted from Kahoua, she miraculously escaped, found Henry and fled across the border to Ivory Coast and on to Guinea, seeking refugee assistance. It was not long before she had to leave Guinea as Liberians there were being stalked and killed. Eventually Kahoua escaped to Bamako, where others from her country had congregated.

As Kahoua shared her story, it was evident that her comfort came from the reality of her knowledge that she belonged to another family, the family of God. Away from home, having experienced tragedy, amidst Christians in a strange country, she had discovered a deeper home.

As Christians we are individuals "on the way," homeward bound, and that makes all the difference to our ability to endure life in the present. In Moscow I met an elderly man, a lay leader in the Russian church, who was nearing the end of his life. He had lived through horrifying experiences in each of the brutal Soviet regimes. His had been an extremely difficult life. Yet as he spoke, there was a degree of spiritual depth and a calmness in his presence that was powerfully moving. When I left him, I recall having the distinct impression that he knew to whom he truly belonged and where he held his true citizenship.

When you are living in a foreign country, when the frustrations seem to become unbearable, thoughts of home or of going home naturally surface. I will never forget the tremendous relief I felt when I was finally sitting on the plane in Kinshasa Airport after having been humiliated by the Zairian soldiers. Even though I had eighteen hours of travel ahead of me, I was going home.

We are resident expatriates but with passports to, with full-blooded citizenship in, a place we have not yet seen. But thanks to John's memory of the vision he received, found in Revelation, we know it is a place where "God himself will be with [us]," and where there will be no more tears, mourning, crying, pain or death; where everything will be made new (Rev 21:1-5).

Elijah, reminded of his true yet unseen citizenship, was encouraged to pull himself together and stop running. It was the refreshment he needed, enabling him to hear the Lord's final call to him to anoint a new generation of political and religious leaders.

Augustine of Hippo, at the age of fifty-six, in the year 410, received the news that Rome had been sacked. In human terms he viewed it as a great tragedy. Nevertheless, he turned his thoughts away from the earthly city that had meant so much to him and toward the city of God. This is a city, he said, that unlike their earthly ones, men did not build and so men could not destroy. How pertinent this was because in the year 430 the Vandals reached the walls of Hippo just after Augustine had died and while his body was awaiting burial. As the apostle Paul said, and Augustine echoed: "Here we have no continuing city, but we seek one to come."

No matter where we live, at home or in other countries, we are expatriates, spiritually speaking. Jesus himself said, "You do not belong to the world, but I have chosen you out of the world" (Jn 15:19). May that be of comfort to us.

A Vision of Heaven
Bring us, O Lord God, at the last awakening into the house and gate of Heaven, to enter into that gate and dwell in that house, where there shall be no darkness nor dazzling, but one equal light; no noise nor silence, but one equal music; no fears nor hopes, but an equal possession; no ends and beginnings, but one equal eternity, in the habitations of your majesty and your glory, world without end.

A prayer by John Donne

Notes

Introduction
[1]From Development Innovations and Networks, found in *Pulse,* 1992.
[2]As quoted in *Occasional Bulletin,* January 1978, pp. 19–28.
[3]From the Iona Community.

Chapter 1: A Deeper Dimension
[1]*Christian History* 7, no. 2 (1988), p. 24.
[2]Anthony Ugolnik, *The Illuminating Icon* (Grand Rapids, Mich.: Eerdmans, 1989), p. 96.
[3]David Porter, *The Practical Christianity of Malcolm Muggeridge* (Downers Grove, Ill.: InterVarsity Press, 1983), p. 83.
[4]Malcolm Muggeridge, *Confessions of a Twentieth-Century Pilgrim* (San Francisco: Harper & Row, 1988), pp. 93–94.

Chapter 2: Keep On Keeping On
[1]Kenneth Cragg, *The Arab Christian* (Louisville, Ky.: Westminster John Knox, 1991), pp. 260–61.
[2]N. S. Ateek, *Justice and Only Justice* (Louisville, Ky.: Westminster John Knox, 1991), p. 184.
[3]J. Carden, *Morning, Noon and Night* (London: Church Missionary Society), n.p.

Chapter 3: Celebrating Life
[1]William Blake, *Songs of Innocence and of Experience* (London: Phoenix, 1996), pp. 55–56.
[2]Malcolm Muggeridge, "The Hope of Christianity," an address given at Wheaton College, Wheaton, Ill., April 5, 1979.

Chapter 4: Rediscovering Jesus Our Teacher
[1]E. Stanley Jones, *Gandhi: Portrayal of a Friend* (Nashville: Abingdon, 1976), p. 55.
[2]Ibid., p. 77.
[3]E. Stanley Jones, *The Christ of the Indian Road* (London: Hodder & Stoughton, 1925), pp. 63–64.
[4]B. H. Steeter and A. J. Appasamy, *The Sadhu: A Study in Mysticism and Practical Religion* (London: Macmillan, 1921).
[5]Mother Teresa, *A Gift for God* (San Francisco: Harper & Row, 1975), p. 53.
[6]Ibid., p. 38.
[7]Louis Fischer, *Gandhi: His Life and Message for the World* (New York: Mentor/New American Library, 1954), p. 131.
[8]Anton Wessels, *Images of Jesus* (Grand Rapids, Mich.: Eerdmans, 1990), p. 128.
[9]A. J. Appasamy, *The Cross in Heaven* (Cambridge: Lutterworth, 1956).
[10]Jones, *Christ of the Indian Road,* p. 37.

[11]Friedrich Heiler, *The Gospel of Sadhu Sundar Singh* (Delhi: ISPCK, 1996), pp. 115–16.

[12]Ibid., pp. 123–24.

[13]Jose Luis Gonzalez-Balado and Janet N. Playfoot, eds., *My Life for the Poor: Mother Teresa of Calcutta* (New York: Ballantine, 1985), p. 114.

[14]Nirod Kumar Biswas, in R. S. Sugirtharajah and Cecil Hargreaves, *Readings in Indian Christian Theology* (London: SPCK, 1993), p. 125.

Chapter 5: An Invitation to Freedom

[1]Richard Gray, *Black Christians and White Missionaries* (New Haven, Conn.: Yale University Press, 1990), p. 5.

[2]Desmond Tutu, from an impromptu address to marchers in "A March for Freedom" demonstration, at St. George's Cathedral, Cape Town, September 2, 1989.

[3]Desmond Tutu, "The Theological Liberation in Africa," *Africa Theology en Route,* 1979, p. 166.

[4]John Mbiti, *African Religions and Philosophy* (London: Heinemann Educational Books, 1969), p. 57.

[5]Cyprian *To Donatus* 1.4.

[6]Vincent J. Donovan, *Christianity Rediscovered* (New York: Orbis, 1991), p. 200.

[7]John Bunyan, *The Pilgrim's Progress* (Westwood, N.J.: Barbour, 1985), pp. 131, 134.

[8]H. R. Rookmaaker, *Modern Art and the Death of a Culture* (London: Inter-Varsity Press, 1970), p. 247.

[9]Veronica Zundel, ed., *The Lion Book of Famous Prayers* (Oxford: Lion, 1983), p. 108.

[10]Martin Luther King Jr., "I Have a Dream," an address given at the Lincoln Memorial in Washington, D.C., August 28, 1963.

Chapter 6: Unboxing God

[1]Rudyard Kipling, "The Ballad of the East and West," 1889.

[2]Choan-Send Song, *Third-Eye Theology: Theology in Formation in Asian Settings* (Maryknoll, N.Y.: Orbis, 1979), pp. 9–12.

[3]Lao Tzu and Victor Mair, trans., *Tao Te Ching* (New York: Bantam, 1990), p. 48.

[4]Megan Gabriel Lanham, *Snatched from the Dragon* (Nashville: Nelson, 1990), pp. 57–61.